No Pie, No Priest

No Pie, No Priest

A JOURNEY THROUGH THE FOLK SPORTS OF BRITAIN

Harry Pearson

**SIMON &
SCHUSTER**

London · New York · Sydney · Toronto · New Delhi

First published in Great Britain by Simon & Schuster UK Ltd, 2023

Copyright © Harry Pearson, 2023

The right of Harry Pearson to be identified as the author of this work has been
asserted in accordance with the Copyright, Designs and Patents Act, 1988.

1 3 5 7 9 10 8 6 4 2

Simon & Schuster UK Ltd
1st Floor
222 Gray's Inn Road
London WC1X 8HB

www.simonandschuster.co.uk
www.simonandschuster.com.au
www.simonandschuster.co.in

Simon & Schuster Australia, Sydney
Simon & Schuster India, New Delhi

A CIP catalogue record for this book is available from the British Library

Hardback ISBN: 978-1-4711-9830-4
eBook ISBN: 978-1-4711-9831-1

Typeset in Bembo by M Rules
Printed and Bound in the UK using 100% Renewable Electricity
at CPI Group (UK) Ltd

CONTENTS

Introduction   1

1   Booting the Barrel   11
2   The Rattle of Stags in Rut   29
3   High Skill and the Rustle of Petticoats   39
4   Knock Her Head Off, Billy   53
5   Buttocking and Velvet   67
6   The Crack of Steel on Bone   81
7   Thunderous Dairy   95
8   Metal Melody   105
9   Never Bet on Anything That Talks   125
10 Cake, Rattle and Bowl   147
11 Big Rocks and Shortbread   165
12 An Uncommon Bias   185
13 Bullets and Bruised Shins   205
14 Cheggies and Alleys   217
15 Tap and Slap   229

Acknowledgements   247

INTRODUCTION

Recently, I was invited to speak to the local Women's Institute. I was delighted to accept because it has long been my contention that a British man or woman who craves entry into a world of the mysterious and bizarre is faced with a simple choice. You can fly to a distant rainforest, paddle up a piranha-stuffed river, hack through snake-infested jungle and then spend a few months with the sort of folk who manufacture a potent alcoholic drink by chewing up leaves and spitting them into a hollow tree; or you can stay at home and read the WI reports in the local paper. ('Members and visitors enjoyed a lively beetle drive followed by pie and peas supper. The prize for the best everyday object shaped like a stoat was won by Mrs Dawkins.')

I put this point to the WI meeting. It was greeted with wry chuckles. WI members have a keen sense of irony. Besides which, you never get much argument when you suggest to British people that they are, perhaps, just a little eccentric. It is the equivalent of telling a Frenchman he's sophisticated.

The British countryside is full of arcane and bewildering things. If you don't believe me, try entering one of the baking competitions at a local agricultural show. This is a place where rituals as meticulous as any Japanese tea ceremony are played out, the exact origins and meanings of which nobody can explain. Why, for example, do show committees of the Industrial Section (Home Baking) insist that scones are entered in fours, while éclairs and meringues need only come in triplicate and a brace of teacakes is considered quite good enough? Is there some socio-economic reason why biscuits in North Yorkshire must be entered by the half dozen, while just four suffice in County Durham? Yet, while nobody is clear why iced buns must be 'in paper wrappers', or the coconut haystacks must be 'egg cup-sized', one thing is certain: you ignore the instructions at your peril. Disqualification and ignominy await those who transgress *The Code*.

Nowadays, the WI runs a course in baking etiquette to avoid such sticky situations. 'I remember the first show I entered,' one of the members confessed as we sat over our tea and dainties at the meeting's end. 'I was ruled ineligible because I'd crimped my sausage rolls instead of concealing the seams.' 'Were they shortcrust?' the woman sitting next to her asked. 'Because you never crimp shortcrust. It's like a savoury quiche. If you were to enter a savoury quiche in a fluted dish you would be disqualified.'

'Why?' I asked.

'Because,' the speaker said matter-of-factly, 'only a sweet flan should be fluted.'

Well, obviously.

The same thing applies to sport. When I was seventeen, I spent two weeks with a Norwegian family. Arild had been at school with me for a year. His father, Einar, had sent him to England to learn the language but also because, he told his son, 'if you spend all your life here in Norway you will never understand why the world is such a big mess'. At the time this seemed rather insulting, though looking back now I can see that if you wanted an insight into human folly, Britain in the 1970s was just the place to get it. After all what other nation had the three-day week, Brentford Nylons *and* Jimmy Hill?

Arild and his family lived in the mountains of Telemark. Their lifestyle was like something out of the 1960s children's TV series *Tales From Europe*, except that it wasn't in black and white. We got up in the morning, had fish pudding and fudge-coloured goat's cheese for breakfast, skied to a nearby lake, fished through holes in the ice and then skied back with the catch, before hanging it from the rafters in the upper floor of a wooden barn so that it could dry in the freezing wind.

It was Easter, a time of great celebration in Norway, and at night we went out with Arild's elder brother, Trond. There were no cafés, bars or hotels in the village, so we loaded up the boot of Trond's battered old Saab with beer and aquavit and drove round and round the icy roads, picking up friends and meeting other people who were doing exactly the same thing, exchanging greetings and passing drinks from car to car. It was fifteen degrees below, so a car boot was as good as a fridge.

One night around midnight, we came across a tractor embedded in a 6-foot snow drift by a T-junction. 'That looks like Knut Sundgot's tractor,' Trond said. He parked the Saab and we all got out and waded into the drift looking for Mr Sundgot. We found him close by the tractor, sunk a metre down into the powdery snow, fast asleep and reeking of alcohol.

We picked him up and carried him back to the car, loaded him in the back seat and set off again. After a few minutes Knut Sundgot woke up. He had been drinking all day at his place up on the hill, he explained after a few reviving chugs of beer, and he had decided to come down to see a few people. 'But I was too plastered to drive my car,' he reasoned with an inebriate's logic, 'so I took the tractor instead.' Unfortunately, the road down from his farm was very long and straight, and he must have fallen asleep at the wheel. 'When did you set off, Mr Sundgot?' Arild asked. 'About nine thirty,' the man replied. He looked at his wristwatch. 'By God,' Knut Sundgot exclaimed. 'One hour longer and I would have died of hypothermia!' And he let out a mighty guffaw and all the other Norwegians in the car joined in, tickled by the thought of so silly and pointless a death.

A similar devil-may-care attitude to physical safety was exhibited at the village festival on Easter Monday. The highlight of this carnival came in mid-afternoon when the villagers took a great barrel that had once been used to store salt herrings and removed the steel bands. Competitors each took a pair of the 4-foot long wooden slats and tied the bottom to his or her boots with leather thongs. Thus equipped, they skied down a very, very steep hill at the bottom of which was a two-metre high ramp. For well over an hour, insensibly drunk Norwegians zoomed down the slope, hit the ramp and somersaulted skywards, landing on their heads in the snow. A huge crowd roared and chuckled. 'Does anybody ever break their neck doing this?' I asked Arild. 'Oh yes,' he said with a big happy grin, 'but not every year, of course.' He saw that I was puzzled. 'Well,' he said, 'I guess in Britain you don't have anything so crazy as this.'

At the time I thought Arild was right. But that was because I wasn't looking at things straight. I was mistaking the normal for the ordinary. It has been said that the medieval Flemish peasant knew only that which he could see from his village church tower. Likewise, rural children in 1960s England knew only the world they could get to on their bicycles. I grew up in a village on the northern edge of the North Yorkshire Moors. If you had asked me when I was ten to name the world's most commonly held religious faith, I would have answered without hesitation 'Methodism'. My knowledge of what sports exercised the bodies and minds of people around the globe was likewise skewed by parochialism. From what I could tell from my travels on an old Raleigh bike with cow-horn handlebars and a right-hand grip regularly lubricated with 3-in-1 oil so I could rev it like the throttle of a speedway bike, the three most popular games on the planet were football, cricket and quoits.

The latter filled summer evenings in the Esk Valley as

surely as midgie clouds filled the moorland skies. Riding through places like Castleton on warm July nights when the day seemed never ending, you'd hear the sharp collision of metal, the wet slap of clay and the comments of the old men in braces who gathered around the ends, breaking off discussions of sheep prices and hernias to offer sage advice in voices that creaked and wheezed like punctured concertinas. To be champion of the Danby Invitation Quoits League seemed, to the childhood me, to be an achievement on a par with winning the British Open golf, or the heavyweight championship of the world.

Decades later, when I mentioned this to a contemporary who grew up in the Sussex countryside, he nodded and replied, 'I would have said the same, only with football, cricket and stoolball.'

'I've never heard of stoolball,' I said.

'Well, I've never heard of quoits,' he answered in a vehement tone. The reply created a slightly peevish atmosphere, but made my point, I guess. People my age brought up in Somerset might have felt the same way about the importance of western skittles, while natives of Kent have been equally adamant about the world-conquering nature of bat-and-trap and those in the Lake District about the hegemony of Cumberland and Westmorland wrestling.

The chink of steel ringer on iron hob, the rattle of *lignum vitae* cheese on elm pins, the snap of oak bat on rubber ball, the rap of metal toe-cap on shinbone, the squelch of velvet trunks on boggy turf . . . From the Middle Ages through to the nineteenth century, these were the sounds of sport in Britain. Yet as tennis, golf, snooker and the rest rose, other games that had once been just as popular were forgotten, left to languish in the backwaters and develop unheeded in the boondocks.

While Victorian public schoolmasters and Oxbridge-educated gentlemen were taming football, codifying cricket, bringing the values of muscular Christianity to the boxing ring and the athletics field, games that dated back to the pagan era clung on in isolated pockets of rural Britain, unmodified by the tastes of future Empire builders, shunned by the media and sport's ruling elites.

In Tudor days, governments had tried to ban sports like quoits and skittles, fearful of their effect on the nation's martial spirit; the Roundheads had attempted to stamp out their joyful, drunken barbarism with their links to eldritch lore and the world of Herne the Hunter; the Victorians moved to shut them down as untamed mob-ruled exhibitions of violence, gambling and encouragers of grievous immorality.

Yet these indigenous games clung tenaciously on, defying commercial trends, societal changes and the intervention of local council health and safety officers – the latter-day equivalent of the Puritans.

And, so, they remain: small, secret worlds, laws unto themselves, free from media hype and VAR controversies, wreathed in an arcane language of face-gaters, whack-ups, sops, potties, sticklers, gates-of-hell and katsticks. They're as much a part of the British countryside as the natterjack toad and the chalkhill blue, and equally as threatened by the modern world.

This book is not about self-consciously zany inventions such as bog-snorkelling and extreme ironing that seem designed to confirm a dearly held belief that while you don't have to be mad to live in Britain, it helps. Nor is it about the weird abandoned sports of yesteryear like ski ballet and aerial golf. It is about traditional sports, centuries-old and deeply rooted, that are still played competitively – often viciously so – in communities across the British Isles.

Rural life in Britain has changed dramatically over the past forty years. Heavy industry in the shape of mines and foundries has all but disappeared, agriculture now employs a quarter of the people it once did, rural schools, shops and post offices have closed, public transport links have been severed. Many of the institutions that once provided focal points for communities have gone.

On many Sunday afternoons in my childhood, my father and I would take my grandmother out for a drive. She rarely spoke, except when our wanderings took us through Kirkleatham in North Yorkshire. Here she would briefly break her silence, point out of the window at a large detached house on the outskirts of the village and say, 'That place used to be a pub.' She said it so often I've come to think of it as one of the great catchphrases of the 1970s.

Back then, you see, it was a novelty for a pub to close down. My dad's best mate at British Steel, Big Roy Gowling, had made a small fortune from investments. 'He only puts his money in two things – public houses and undertakers,' my father would say admiringly of his friend's financial cunning, 'He says there are only two things you can be certain of: men will always drink beer and they will always die.'

Big Roy proved the latter point himself several decades ago, and as well he did, really, otherwise he might be facing fiscal ruin. At present, an average of four British public houses close down every day. That's the highest rate since the 1904 Compensation Act forced 10 per cent of the nation's licensed premises to shut in a single year. Most pubs never reopen, converted instead to residential or retail use.

For sport in rural communities, that can be a big problem. While it's common for elite sportsmen to speak dismissively of teams playing 'like a pub side', the fact is that licensed premises have been a focal point in British sport for centuries. The nation's first great cricket team, the Hambledon Club in Hampshire, was run out of the Bat & Ball inn at Broadhalfpenny Down by the landlord Richard Nyren, and across the country tens of thousands of sides – in games that range from rugby to darts – are centred around pubs. And pubs are disappearing from the landscape as surely as hedgehogs and hawkmoths.

The global pandemic that raged through the country like some vengeful spectre compounded the damage. Clubs and leagues folded. Events were postponed temporarily and then forever. Yet sport, in its often weird and forgotten forms, clung on. Those featured in these pages are far removed – and not just geographically – from the great sporting institutions of Britain, from Lord's, Wembley, the Principality Stadium, Murrayfield, Silverstone and Wimbledon. Yet, in many ways, the role these sports play is even more important. In small communities, they provide social cohesion, a core around which people can weave the threads of everyday life – childhood, youth, work, friendships, family. Despite the lure of television and the internet, they remain at the heart of things. They are a reminder that the way to happiness is not success on a global scale, but the taking of pleasure in your surroundings and joy in the everyday.

1

Booting the Barrel

THE HAND BA' GAME, RUTLAND

A few weeks after the third lockdown ended, I'd gone to watch Carlisle United play, along with a friend of mine who is a doctor. As we stood in a packed and heaving pub, filled with stag and hen parties from Workington and Whitehaven, belly laughs and cackling reverberating around the walls and the air thick with moisture and celebrity-endorsed scents, my friend said, 'Look at this. You know, all those months of masks and isolation and shielding – in three months the world will have forgotten all about it.'

I disagreed. The whole thing had been so momentous, I imagined I'd go on talking about it for the rest of my life, like my parents' generation did about the Second World War. To me, it appeared inevitable that in thirty years' time when I said, 'But of course you don't remember what it was like back when they'd only allow one person per household to buy a four-pack of toilet roll,' young people would wrinkle their noses and roll their eyes, like I had done when my dad said, 'You wouldn't be turning your nose up at a bruised banana if you'd ever had a ration-book.'

But by the time 2021 ended, I could see that my friend had been right. COVID-19 now seemed like some strange dream, the memories of it recoverable only in fragments. My abiding memory was a trip to Middlesbrough during the second lockdown. During the first, a Teesside bus driver had told me the town looked like 'a zombie apocalypse, only without the zombies'. Ten months later, if anything the scene was even more baleful. The only shops with lights on were the pawn-brokers and the sole person I saw was pacing furiously up and down by the Middlesbrough College 'trim trail and events area' carrying out a bitter argument with an invisible foe. In the underpass at the station, the police posters warning against anti-social drinking seemed like mementos of gladder days.

In the supermarket where I went to buy a sandwich, one of the automated cash-outs was malfunctioning. 'Do you wish to continue?' a robotic female voice asked. 'Do you wish to continue? . . . Do you wish to continue? . . .' On another afternoon, you would have bet on hearing a growling voice reply, 'All things considered, luv, no I fucking don't.' But that day, in the anxious emptiness, even Teesside had no cynicism left to offer. Later, I realised that wearing a mask at the checkout made me load my bag in the style of a bank-robber stuffing cash into a holdall in an episode of *The Sweeney*.

Most of the other memories had evaporated, though. Social

bubbles, R numbers and elbow bumps had all vanished from my conscience as rapidly as video stores, audio cassettes and fax machines. The debris of those grim years remained in the council social distancing signs tied to lampposts, the shadows of gaffer tape arrows left on the carpets of pubs, and the brackets that had once held hand-sanitiser by the entry to shops. I imagine that at some point in the future we will have to explain these to our grandchildren as our grandparents once did to us such arcane mysteries as mounting blocks, weathervanes and sun dials. 'What?' they will respond incredulously. 'So some people carried, like, a two-metre long stick so you couldn't get too close to them? That's mad.'

COVID had gone, or rather we had learned to live with it, so now here I was on the train down to the East Midlands, mask-less and free at last from the seminal stickiness of antiseptic spray.

The train was running forty minutes late due to 'line equipment failure in the Retford area'. Perhaps it was my age but the more the customer services manager repeated this phrase, the more it sounded to me like a euphemism for erectile dysfunction. The lateness of the train was, of course, compensated for by the fact that there was a 'dedicated at-seat trolley service' on the train. I wondered what had happened to the undedicated at-seat trolley service and concluded it had likely got off at Doncaster and was now smoking weed in an underpass.

I was going to Leicestershire – meeting a friend in Melton Mowbray and then heading to Hallaton for one of the English countryside's great sporting events. Despite the Retford business, I arrived in the town a little early and went for a saunter while I waited for my mate. Melton Mowbray had given the world three great foodstuffs. Two of them were cheese: Red Leicester and Stilton. I was looking at the other.

'Best pies in the world, Melton Mowbray,' the old man standing beside me said. He had an East Midlands accent so flat you could have slid it under a door. He had seen me staring in the window of Dickinson & Morris on Nottingham Street, which billed itself as Ye Olde Pork Pie Shoppe, and, evidently in want of conversation, had decided to join me. He was barking up the wrong tree, though. I made a non-committal response and moved away. When it comes to pies, I am sensitive. You see, my family was once savagely divided by what can only be described as an internecine savoury pastry war.

There were other culinary stand-offs, admittedly. My dad's family were committed to Hoe's relish and Pan Yan pickle, while my mum's would entertain only Hammonds' Yorkshire sauce and Branston. Many a trip to the seaside ended in an acrimonious dispute over the merits of favourite chip shops and, when it came to beer, the impossibility of finding a pub that served both Theakston's Old Peculier and Vaux Samson meant we often went out together and then sat in pubs several streets apart. It was the pork pies that were the cause of the bitterest trouble, though. When it came to them it was the King vs Parliament, Mods vs Rockers, Mary Berry vs Paul Hollywood. There was no compromise.

My grandfather and his brothers, George and Joe, grew up in Middlesbrough. As lads they had pledged pie-allegiance to a well-known local maker when they were still wearing short trousers. They were steadfast. While Joe and George stayed in the town, my grandfather married a girl from the coast and settled there. Later, his daughter, my mother, moved to a North Yorkshire village that had a butcher's in it that was so famous for its pork pies that on Saturday mornings there'd be a queue 50 yards long outside. They had to limit each customer to two pies each to prevent a riot. And that was when the trouble started, because our house was 50 yards from this meat-jelly-and-pastry paradise.

At some point my grandfather was lured into buying a pork pie from the village butcher and pretty soon they were the only pork pies he'd eat. He might have stayed silent on the matter but, like a man recently alerted to the existence of God by a burning bush, he just couldn't keep the good news to himself. He became evangelical on the topic.

It all kicked off round my great-grandmother's one Christmas Eve nearly half a century ago. She lived in a tiny terraced house, the living room so small the only way all of us could fit in was with kids sitting on knees and menfolk arranged shoulder-to-shoulder around the walls. We all had our place. You could tell where the men stood even when they weren't there by the height of the stains that their brilliantine hair oil left on the woodchip.

At some point my great-gran expressed the view that a nice pork pie would do her for lunch on New Year's Day.

'You want to have a one from our Pam's village,' my grandad announced.

'What are you talking about?' Uncle Joe said. 'Have you gone screwy? I'll get her a one from in town.'

'The only thing she's getting from you is a load of baloney,' my grandad replied.

By this stage my mother had started to wrestle me into my coat and signalled for my dad to go out and get the engine of our Morris Oxford turning over. She had spent a lifetime in the company of these men. She knew fighting talk when she heard it.

Things might have stayed at a rolling simmer, but at this point my grandma's sister's husband, who hailed from out in the moorlands where – or so my grandfather said – the people were so backward they called the train an iron horse, started in. Uncle Lenny had a voice so loud and gravelly it sounded like an explosion in a flint mine. Now he boomed out his opinion that the pork pies from the butcher near the foundry where he worked knocked all other pork pies on God's green earth into the middle of next week.

What happened next I cannot honestly say, for my mum had hustled me out the door. From reports it seemed the coppers got things under control quite quickly once they arrived on the scene.

Having evaded a similar fracas with the old man on Nottingham Street, I headed to the pub my friend and I had arranged to meet at. Pies were definitely on my mind, because they were an essential part of the great event I had come to see. It was Easter Monday and I was heading for Hallaton and the annual Hare Pie Scramble and Bottle Kicking. The event had been cancelled for two years because of COVID, but now it was back.

According to *The Percy Anecdotes* – a collection of titbits from the *Star* newspaper compiled by a Scots patent agent, Sholto Percy, and first published in 1820 – the Hallaton Hare Pie Scramble and Bottle Kicking came about when 'an eccentric inhabitant of Hallaton bequeathed a piece of land to the rector of the town' and in trust provided funds to furnish 'two hare pies, a quantity of ale and two dozen penny loaves to be scrambled for on Easter Monday'. The eccentric apparently did this because he was 'ambitious that his memory should be preserved'. Since no one now seems to know the singular benefactor's name, we may conclude that his aim was thwarted.

In his book *In Search of Food* David Mabey says the origins of the hare pie scramble dated far back to the 'symbolic sacrifice and celebration of Easter through its sacred creature, the hare'. Hunting hares at Easter was a custom in Leicester up until the end of the eighteenth century, though even then it was more symbolic – a trail hunt through the city using the corpse of a dead cat. Likewise, the pie at Hallaton wasn't made with hare, but with beef, pork or mutton.

Like the pork pie in my own family, the hare pie in Hallaton had been the source of fractious violence. In 1790, a new rector, the Reverend T. C. Bewicke, had refused to supply a pie for the event which he believed had heathen origins. With the symbolism of the hare and its links to the pagan fertility rites of spring, plus the fact some believed Hare Pie Bank where the scramble took place had been a sacred site in the Iron Age, perhaps he was fearful it might all end with the villagers burning him alive in a wicker man. As it was, that nearly happened anyway. No sooner had the vicar made his proclamation against the pies than posters started appearing around Hallaton: 'No pie, no priest and a job for the glazier' (some claim the message was written on the rectory door in blood). Fearful of a brick through the window or worse, Reverend Bewicke relented, bought the pies and the event went ahead.

The scramble was originally held on a piece of land called Harecrop Leys, but after a series of Enclosures in 1770, it was moved to the field where it's still held today. The scramble is really nothing more than a food fight; it's the bottle-kicking that had attracted me to Rutlandshire. The game was played between the men of Hallaton and those of the nearby village of Medbourne and, according to the *Leicester Daily Post* of 1914, was often 'taken advantage of to settle scores between the villagers'.

The bottle-kicking was one of a whole series of annual football matches played around Britain. Most took place earlier in the year. While for most people Shrove Tuesday is a time to whip up pancake batter and squeeze some lemons, in towns and villages from Cornwall to the Scottish Borders, its arrival sees shopkeepers board up their windows and citizens stuff their socks with cardboard. For Shrovetide is the day that the majority of Britain's traditional mass 'football' matches take place, raucous, rough affairs that trace their origins back to the Norman Conquest and the Breton game of *soule*.

The games – sometimes called hand ba', or hurling (though no sticks are used) – were played all over the British country-side until nineteenth-century moralists began to have them outlawed. As a consequence of this clampdown, thousands of annual mass games were abolished and now barely a dozen remain. Given that in one notorious Georgian encounter between the Men of Suffolk and the Men of Norfolk on Diss Common it was reported that nine participants died, some may judge this to be for the best. However, there's also little doubt that our sturdy ancestors, seeing their yearly fun curtailed simply to save the odd life or two, muttered the Victorian equivalent of 'It's health and safety gone daft, is this!'

Though they may resemble a mini-riot, Britain's Pancake Day matches are what would eventually become modern-day football – both association and rugby. Not that followers of Manchester United or Harlequins would recognise much sim-ilarity. The three sports do have some things in common: the ball, for instance, though even that is a loose connection. For the ball in the hand ba' game varies in shape, weight and size, from the cork-filled type used at Ashbourne in Derbyshire to the huge water-filled variety used at Atherstone in Lancashire (which looks more like a cheese than anything Cristiano Ronaldo might dribble), via the moss-packed leather-bound version found at Jedburgh, where they'd originally used an Englishman's severed head.

There are two teams, of course. But eleven or fifteen is insufficient for a true game of hand ba' where opposing sides – usually from different parts of the town, though in Duns in the Scottish Borders they play Married vs Singles – of hundreds are common. Spectators often join in a contest that can run on for many, many hours and, in the absence of floodlighting, often concludes in pitch darkness, the whereabouts of the ball a mystery even to those who are standing a few yards from it.

There are goals too, though only those at Alnwick in Northumberland bear much resemblance to the sets at Wembley or Twickenham, and even these have more in common with a garden arch than either. To score a goal (or hail as it is sometimes called) in hand ba', a player generally has to touch the ball against a designated object (in Duns, one of the 'goals' is a church pulpit) or carry it across a line (usually a parish boundary). In some games, such as in Atherstone, possession of the ball when the clock strikes five is all that matters.

The pitch is not something that would fit into a soccer or rugby stadium, either. At Ashbourne, the goals – a pair of stone plinths embedded into the banks of the River Henmore – are 3 miles apart; at St Columb Major in Cornwall, the playing area often extends to 25 square miles.

There are no referees or touch judges here (though at Alnwick there's an umpire with a bugle instead of a whistle), and certainly no fourth official. The ball can be kicked, thrown, punched or carried – or, in some cases, hidden up a jumper or under a coat and smuggled past unwitting opponents, a piece of subterfuge even Diego Maradona might have stopped short of.

Though there appear no tactics for the pundits to analyse (one early commentator, Daniel Defoe, called a game he watched in Cornwall 'brutish and furious'), the game requires skill, strength, cunning and local knowledge. And while it may not look glamorous, it's worth bearing in mind that, since folk football is part of the tradition of Mardi Gras, two mobs of men fighting over possession of a ball in a freezing, muddy river in Derbyshire is the British equivalent of the Rio Carnival.

It was bright, warm and sunny in Hallaton, a neat little village of pretty thatched cottages with an ivy-wreathed vicarage that looked so appealingly French, I suspected they might have used it as the mayor's house in the 1970s BBC TV adaptation of *Clochemerle* (though possibly the fact that pastry was on my mind and the mayor of that fictional French town was named Piechut had falsely influenced me). By the time I arrived, the bottles had already attended the morning service at the Church of St Michael and All Angels, the pies had been blessed by the vicar and a large crowd had gathered around the pyramid-shaped butter cross at the centre of the village. A brass band played, flags were waved in the air and a man who was dressed like Vincent Price in Roger Corman's *The Masque of the Red Death* wandered around waving a staff for reasons that remained opaque.

After half an hour of unfocused hubbub, a slightly

incongruous group of bagpipers turned up and skirled away as the bottles processed through the town to the kick-off point on Hare Pie Hill. I should say that the bottles are not made of glass but are, in fact, small wooden kegs bound with iron. These were evidently the sort of barrels used by local farmworkers to take their refreshment out into the fields with them. Since each one contains seven pints of ale, you may judge that little farm work got done after lunch in this part of the world, though I'm sure that was by no means the case.

The players were a beefy, rugged bunch, who might have formed several formidable rugby league teams. They marched up the street looking as fierce as men whose toddlers have just been woken by a car alarm. On the fringe of the village, the bagpipers gave way to a male duo doing covers of songs by The Killers, which given the bottle-kicking's violent reputation seemed appropriate.

I walked up the hill with a milling crowd of people dressed for a ramble and took up a position under a large sycamore tree. The countryside around Hallaton was carefully cultivated, sunken lanes ran through pasture lands edged with dark, skeletal hedges. The pastoral loveliness appeared untouched by time. If a regiment of Civil War cavalry in plumed hats and breastplates were to have suddenly galloped across it, they would hardly have looked out of place. Mind you, even Prince Rupert would have given way to the bottle-kickers, whose game commenced when a man in a red-and-white hooped rugby shirt, who possessed the powerful shrieking voice of a drill sergeant-major, hurled one of the bottles in the air. When it hit the ground, an almighty ruck ensued, the like of which I had not seen since I made the mistake of going into the cosmetics department of the Newcastle branch of Fenwick on Christmas Eve.

As I say, the bottles are actually barrels and nobody seems to kick them (and since, filled with beer they weigh 13 pounds apiece, that's likely a good thing), but apart from that, the description of the game is accurate. The aim of the bottle-kicking is to carry, knock or shove the bottles across the two brooks that mark the boundary of the field, carting it through thorn hedges and across barbed wire fences along the way. The game is played 'best of three bottles' and generally lasts for between two and three hours. Nowadays the players number in the dozens, but in the years between the two world wars, the game often involved teams of over 250 per side.

Originally only men from Hallaton took part in the bottle-kicking, which seems to have been more a ceremony than a game, but gradually they were joined, or rather opposed, by the inhabitants of Medbourne 2 miles to the south, who had turned up at some point intent on carrying off the beer-filled barrels for themselves. Soon the Hallatonians had been bolstered by men from nearby villages such as Slawston and Horninghold, while Medbourne had called on re-inforcements from villages to the south, such as Cottingham. Later they'd be joined by Scottish steelworkers from the blast furnaces of Corby.

In 1878, when a railway was being built through Hallaton, the local council attempted to dissuade the villagers from their barbaric pastime by offering to pay for new playing fields if the event was consigned to history. The villagers refused the offer. Any thought that the arrival of the steam age might see the bottle-kicking disappear in a puff of smoke were mistaken. While the line was under construction, the numbers playing the game were swelled by Irish navvies who were laying the track. When the railway opened in 1882, special trains were laid on to bring spectators and players to the event from across the East Midlands.

By the 1890s, the bottle-kicking was a full-blown battle between the two teams. Back in 1796, the writer John Tailby had noted 'a scene of noise and confusion' in which 'bloody noses and bruised fingers' were a hazard. By the turn of the twentieth century, it was a good deal less genteel than that.

When it came to the playing field, Medbourne were at a severe disadvantage as they had to attack up a steep hill and carry the bottle about five times further than the Hallatonians. This is perhaps why it took them until 1929 to register their first point, and until 1936 to record their first victory. To prove it was no fluke, they repeated the feat the following year, causing a great deal of hand-wringing in Hallaton where questions were raised about the diminishing quality of the local menfolk.

One man who didn't take Hallaton's double defeat lightly was arguably the greatest bottle-kicker in history, Fred 'Sporty' Payne. Sporty Payne was a native of Hallaton. He'd driven a tank in the First World War, been awarded the Military Medal for gallantry and promoted to corporal 'in the field'. Photos show a stocky, dapper man with the square jaw of a comic-book action hero. And that is likely not so wide of the mark, since Sporty was pretty much superhuman. By most accounts he had made his debut in the bottle-kicking as a teenager in 1910. He'd taken some hard knocks over the years, too. In 1931, he'd suffered two broken ribs and on another occasion his neck had – by his own account – been dislocated and 'popped back in' by a local vet, the doctor being unavailable. Sporty went into retirement several times but always came back when Hallaton needed him most. In 1940, for example, he returned to the fray wearing his lucky football jersey. At the end of a massive three-hour scrimmage, with his shirt in tatters and two of his teeth broken, Sporty carried the bottle across the Medbourne brook to give Hallaton victory. The villagers cheered and chanted his name. His team mates carried him home on their shoulders. They hoisted him onto the butter cross at the centre of the village as a mark of honour and handed him one of the ale-filled barrels to drink from. 'He has the pluck of twenty men,' said the *Market Harborough Advertiser*, while the *Leicester Daily Post* recorded that Sporty's fame was such that he had been 'mentioned on BBC radio commentary' while 'his photograph has been frequently seen in the London newspapers'.

In 1951, Sporty, evidently bored with life between Easter Mondays, issued a bottle-kicking challenge to any group of men in Leicestershire who were bold enough to take on the Hallaton men in an exhibition match. The *Leicester Evening Mail* reported that two well-known boxers, Len Gardner and

Dick Kelly from Market Harborough, had accepted. 'I have taken part in several Hallaton bottle-kicking scrambles and consider the game the toughest sport in the world,' said Kelly. 'There are no rules in the Hallaton game, but Mr Gardner and I want Mr Payne to agree to a rule disallowing shin-kicking and ear-pulling.'

Sporty, unsurprisingly, responded in the negative. Such restrictions, he said, would neuter the event. He had no wish to see his beloved bottle-kicking 'end up looking like a child's wrestling match'. Fearful for their legs and lugs, the Market Harborough men withdrew from the contest.

By 1957, Sporty was in his sixties and had finally stopped taking part in the bottle-kicking, though his son, Jim, was still a player. It was a time of Medbourne domination (they won every year between 1948 and 1967) and Sporty didn't take it well. Like many retired athletes, he professed himself disgusted with the new generation, claiming that 'a nasty, mean, bitterness has crept in' to the event and that in that year's contest 'fists were used before the teams even got to the bank'. Sporty shook his head at the display of vindictive savagery and wondered what had happened to the days when men could 'give and take a knock-out decently'.

Sporty would surely have approved of the efforts of the modern-day players, who swirled and grunted, yelled and shoved their way down the bank with minimum skulduggery. Some of the fields nearby had lately been the subject of muckspreading, adding a pungent country odour to the whole affair. 'Breathe it in, boy. Clears your tubes, doesn't it?' my Welsh grandmother would have called out at anyone who protested at the pong.

Beyond the slow movement of the mob, the game was hard to follow. It was a mass rolling maul that occasionally collapsed in a heap of limbs, so that it looked like a consortium of drunken octopi playing Twister, though not much like it, admittedly. That the bottle was down there somewhere seemed a matter of faith. It reminded me of one of those 1970s rugby union matches in which, if they'd removed the ball, the players would have carried on rucking in the mud without the slightest loss of focus or pleasure.

After several hours Hallaton triumphed 2-0. Glasses were raised by the butter cross and songs of victory – mainly 'Olé Olé Olé' – were sung in the fading light of evening. The game had survived COVID as surely as it had officious councillors and pious priests.

2

The Rattle of Stags in Rut

SHINTY, SCOTLAND

The last time I had been in Kingussie, it had been so cold that even the air had goosebumps. Almost everything was shut, including the promising-looking Waltzing Waters Aquatheatre, which boasted of having 'the world's most elaborate water, light and music production' which it claimed (and who was I to disagree?) was 'the very finest of its kind in Europe'. That had been back in the winter of 2000. I had vowed to return and, twenty-two years later, I had finally made it. It was considerably warmer than on my last visit, though unhappily the Waltzing Waters had closed down in 2011 and been shipped off to County Kerry. Even if it had been open, I wasn't sure I'd have had time to visit as I had come up just for the day to see Kingussie play Newtonmore in shinty's celebrated Badenoch derby. I was so excited that I felt that when I went to the loo I'd pee soda water.

In 2000 I'd travelled up to the Cairngorms for the same reason: to watch shinty. The temperature was below freezing even at midday and snow clouds hovered over the Cairngorms like the threat of tears above a wedding. I was worried I might have travelled in vain, but the hotel receptionist was reassuring. 'So long as they can see from the goal to the half-way line, they'll play,' she said, cheerily, 'They're tough, the shinty boys.'

True enough. Shinty is a swashbuckling sport, the game Errol Flynn might have engaged in between pirate movies. It is the sport of the Scottish Highlands, played between clubs with evocative names – Glenurquhart, Caberfeidh, Lochaber – at poetically monikered venues – Parc nan Laoch, Eilean Bheannchair – with spectacular views of white-capped peaks and glimmering lochs. The website of the Camanachd Association is the most stirringly written of any sport governing body on the planet. Shinty it says is 'the sport of the curved stick' which pits 'clan against clan, parish against parish, brae against strath'. Just reading it was enough to make you paint your face blue and invade England.

For some reason that I have never quite fathomed, I played shinty at my primary school outside Middlesbrough, a place with altogether less romantic scenery, unless you go all misty-eyed at the sight of a chemical plant. Giving twenty-two kids from Teesside sticks and encouraging them to swing them through the air was a bold decision from our teacher, the jolly Miss Thom, but it paid off. We loved the game, and I believe that if you ever get a chance to watch a match, you will love it too.

Twenty years ago, shinty was still played in the winter, but shortly after, like rugby league, it was moved to the summer months, which among other things made it far less hazardous for away teams travelling to fixtures. This produced howls of outrage from traditionalists who saw it as a sign that every-one – even the shinty boys – had gone soft. At the time of my last visit, Kingussie Camanachd, the self-styled 'Kings of Shinty', were well on their way to the eighth of twenty consecutive league titles – a world record for any sport. The men from the Dell are just about the most successful team in British sport. Formed in the reign of Queen Victoria and financially supported during their early years by the splen-didly named Count de Serra Largo of Tarlogie, the men in red-and-blue's undefeated run had lasted longer than an eat-as-much-as-you-want buffet lunch with Mr Creosote. The last time they had been beaten was in June 1996. Since then they have they have achieved the grand slam of Premiership, MacTavish, Camanachd and Macaulay Cups three times, an appetite for quadruples not seen north of the border since Jim Baxter moved to Sunderland.

The narrowness of shinty's home turf shouldn't fool anyone into thinking that Kingussie's trophy haul has been easily gathered. This is a highly competitive game, the hick-ory and ash sticks, or caman, colliding with such force they set spectators' teeth rattling. Shinty was described by one Victorian English writer as 'a barbarian form of cricket', which was about as accurate as calling rugby union 'croquet for hooligans'. If shinty was a barbarian form of anything, it was hockey, except of course that there is nothing remotely civilised about hockey, as any adolescent boy who has ever thought it would be a laugh to join in with the girls' U16 practice will tell you. I still have the dents. As shinty.com puts it, shinty is 'the ancient sport of stick and ball, where no quarter is asked and none given'.

Despite the obvious attractions of Kingussie, in 2000 I chose not to go to the Dell and watch Kingussie and their star forward, Ronald Ross, whose 1,000-goal career had earned him the nickname 'The Ronaldo of the Glens' (after the original goofy Brazilian Ronaldo, not the later preening Portuguese version), instead travelling a few miles by bus to the Eilan in Newtonmore. I made this decision partly because Newtonmore were playing Ballachulish, a team that played in red to honour the early socialists who'd founded the club, but mainly because the president of Newtonmore, Sir Thomas Macpherson, had once escaped from a Nazi POW camp on a motorcycle, thus unwittingly becoming the inspiration for Steve McQueen's character in *The Great Escape* – one of my childhood idols. Going AWOL from German prison camps was, I should say, something of a specialism of shinty players. Fort William's James 'Ginger' Wilson had successfully escaped from one in 1940 and, speaking his native Gaelic in a successful bid to convince those who stopped him that he was actually Russian, made it all the way across occupied France and into Spain.

On the walk from the bus stop to the ground, I passed a house where one of the Newtonmore players was warming up, slapping the ball against an up-and-over garage door with furious power and then catching the rebound on his stick with the soft delicacy of somebody cradling an egg. It was like watching that memorable tussle between the South African fast bowler Allan Donald and England opening batsman Mike Atherton, only the shinty boy was playing both roles.

Newtonmore's ground was beautifully located along the banks of the Spey and the game was terrific. The ball was blasted about and the curved wooden sticks cleaved the heavy air like claymores. 'Do a lot of people get injured playing this?' I said to the bundle of clothes standing next to me. 'Not at all, not at all,' the man inside them replied in a Highland accent that wasn't so much lilting as capering o'er hill and dale. 'For yourself now, it would be dangerous, naturally. But these lads have played since they left the cradle. They can anticipate the flight of the ball and the movement of the sticks as surely as . . .' At which point our conversation was interrupted by the dull thunk of wood on skull and cries of 'Doctor, doctor!' from the pitch.

The player, whose Ballachulish shirt thankfully hid the gore, was led from the field, blood spurting from a gash above his eye that flapped like a second mouth, while various members of the crowd helpfully endeavoured to remember the number of the local GP. By the time they had formulated something likely from the half-a-dozen different suggestions offered, the wounded man was speeding away to the nearest casualty department in the back of a Ford Sierra.

Shinty fans assured me that such injuries are a rarity.

Perhaps so, though the fact that famous players down the years have included the likes of Dave 'Brick' MacArthur, Hugh 'Horse' Cameron and Dave 'Tarzan' Ritchie, suggests that the shinty field is hardly a place for the velvet-slippered aesthete.

Kingussie's long unbeaten run had eventually been ended by Fort William in 2006, but since then they'd continued to dominate the sport. Today they were playing their arch rivals, my old favourites Newtonmore (who'd had a revival since I'd watched them, winning their first title in twenty-five years in 2010 and remaining competitive ever since). It was derby match, one that was so fiercely contested it once had to be abandoned after a pitch invasion – and that had been back in 1934 when people behaved themselves.

The Dell was tucked away in a curve of the Spey amid a rough meadow filled with cow parsley. It had the look of a lower-tier non-league football ground, the pitch ringed with advertising hoardings, a timber clubhouse along one touch-line and a small covered stand of seats. A crowd of a couple of hundred had gathered as the two teams were led out onto the field by a lone bagpiper.

The game was in the MOWI Premiership and though it was still early in the season, both sides looked in with a chance of lifting the trophy. The 'throw-up' was at 3 p.m., the grey-clad ref lofting the white ball 12 feet into the sky and the caman of the leaping players clattering.

Shinty is a bit like ice hockey in the sense that you don't have to really understand the subtleties of the rules or tactics to enjoy the spectacle. There are twelve players on each team.

A game lasts ninety minutes. If the ball is struck into the goal, it's called a hail and worth one point. Players can stop the ball with their feet or shins (called cleeking), but only if it doesn't rebound more than a stick's length. What would be throw-ins in football are called shys, the ball thrown in the air and struck two-handed with an axe-like swing. There are no restrictions on how high the caman can be raised, or the ball struck. And that's about all you need to know, really.

The game between Kingussie and Newtonmore was played at a gallop, the ball flying from one end of the 150-yard-long pitch to the other, the players scurrying around non-stop with the energy of spaniels quartering a field. Kingussie struck early, James Falconer smashing the ball in from about 18 yards with just five minutes gone. 'Come on, boys!' a woman standing near me bellowed, with a voice that sounded like gravel in a blender. 'Let's keep working!' a fellow to her left called, in the mellifluous tones of a curlew. 'How many more times, referee?' moaned a man to my right, who might have been the brother of Private Fraser from *Dad's Army*.

There were tussles and collisions and fifty-fifty challenges of such violence they would have made a blind man wince. The players jinked and twisted, occasionally stopping in mid-flight to control a hard-hit pass with their feet. The action barely paused. In the twenty-second minute, Kingussie went two up. A quick break down the right ended with Roddy Young bringing down an aerial cross with his stick, outwitting a defender and cracking in a shot from a tight angle.

I felt some pity for the shinty goalkeepers standing in the

middle of their giant 12-feet-by-10-feet goals. They wore neither helmets nor masks, and they didn't have the big leg pads that protect hockey keepers. The ball flew towards them at tremendous speeds and all they had to stop it was their caman. They looked like men who had walked into a cricket net to face a bowling machine set at 80mph, wearing their street clothes and armed with a walking stick. That both custodians pulled off a series of saves was a minor miracle of alertness, athleticism and courage.

The Kingussie keeper got some of his own back on the outfield players a few minutes later, rushing out of his penalty box to chop down an on-rushing Newtonmore attacker. The resulting free-hit came to nothing, but thirty seconds later the ball found its way to Iain Robinson who whacked it home, the ball sizzling into the net at such speed it was a wonder it didn't burst into flames.

When half-time came, I went for a stroll around the pitch to catch my breath. Shinty, as you might expect, has a history that stretches back into the mists of time. Even though the first formal shinty club had been founded at Aberdeen University in 1861, as late as the 1880s the game was still being played on pitches that could be a quarter of a mile long, by teams of upwards of twenty-two men per side and featuring the sort of mass carnage that would have made even Sporty Payne flinch. The Society of True Highlanders had issued a set of rules in 1870, the Glasgow Celtic Association another in 1879 and Captain Chisholm of Glassburn had published his in 1880. However, it was an historic game at the Dell between Kingussie and Glasgow Cowal that really sparked the move to a fully agreed-upon set of rules. The Camanachd Association was founded shortly afterwards here in Kingussie and has been stewarding the game ever since.

The second half proceeded at the same breakneck speed as the first. Kingussie added to their lead after a swift move down the visitors' left culminated with Savio Genini, a twenty-five-year-old gamekeeper, driving home from 15 yards.

It was Robinson, again, who brought the away team back into it. The attacker had dislocated a shoulder in the opening season fixture against Kinlochshiel, but he was evidently back to peak form. He tackled a Kingussie defender, wrestled his way past him and slammed the ball high into the goal. Stocky, with dark hair and beard, Robinson bore a resemblance to battling Italian midfielder Gennaro Gattuso. He played a bit like him, too, snapping into challenges with the abandon of a man joy-riding in a stolen body. He got the equaliser and his hat-trick nine minutes from time.

The sixth goal was the signal for me to race off back to the station and the last train south that would get me home before Sunday. As I walked away, I could hear the clash of the sticks echoing across the valley. The sound is so ruggedly elemental that in autumn it's said that the clattering of the caman sometimes attracts red deer stags who, mistaking it for the clashing antlers of their rivals-in-rut, turn up on the touchline, myopic with lust and searching for a fight. From what I'd seen at the Dell, I'd have taken odds on any of the shinty boys to fell the Monarch of the Glen inside a minute.

3

High Skill and the Rustle of Petticoats

STOOLBALL, SUSSEX

Back when I was at college in London, I lived near an all-girls private day school. On Wednesday afternoons, the students played netball on a court that was overlooked by the street and a row of terraced houses. You could always tell when a netball match was in progress because the pavement and the upper windows of the houses were dotted with furtive-looking middle-aged men in rainwear. Seeing these sad old fools ogling the sixth formers in their aertex shirts and canvas skirts, I would be overcome by a wave of disgust. How pathetic, I would think, as I passed them.

Something of that loathing has lingered. And now I was a lone and lanky middle-aged man and I was about to go and watch young women playing sport. *It is for research,* I told myself. *I am a sportswriter and I am quite capable of appreciating women athletes for their athletic prowess alone.* All of which was perfectly true, yet still, somewhere in the back of my mind, my teenage self sneered back, *Yeah, right, Grandad. Better take your pac-a-mac.*

I therefore approached Glynde Recreation Ground in a sort of skulking manner, which, it gradually dawned on me, made me look far more like the 1980s hockey-watchers than was necessary. I took out my notebook and pen, and tried to look as business like as possible. The game I'd come to watch was an early-season fixture in the Sussex Stoolball Association Mid Division (Ladies).

I should add that stoolball had suffered its fair share of this kind of prurient attention over the years. An article in the *Evening Standard* in 1909 by a writer named Tindal gave an account of a match at Glynde that was a pretty clear indication of what the female athlete was up against then, as now. After first 'hazarding a guess' that stoolball was the only game ever invented by women, Tindal went off on a fantasy riff about merry milkmaids before describing the game he had witnessed: 'Pretty faces, lithe forms, rippling petticoats and flashing ankles – to these attractions were added inconceivable skill in catching and throwing, smart fielding and batting.' That he got away without any of the players smacking him across the head with a bat is surely testament to their forbearance.

Unhappily, Mr Tindal was not alone among male reporters in taking this lubricious attitude to stoolball. To the Victorian patriarchy, the sport seemed to lurk somewhere between the Gentlemen versus Players match at Lord's and a private production of Oscar Wilde's *Salome*. Class prejudice played its part in the reports too, for while the upper-class ladies were praised for their nimble grace and the flush of rosy colour on their creamy cheeks, the players of less noble backgrounds were generally mocked for their bumbling incompetence. They were brainless, sweating duffers who were always likely to attempt to catch a flying ball in their skirts, even though that was strictly against the rules. Being attracted to the sister of the chatelaine was one thing, but for the middle-class nineteenth-century English male to confess a pang of longing for the scullery maid was quite beyond the pale. The 'rustics' were strictly for comic relief only.

In truth, though, stoolball seems to have had frisky associations from its early days, with Restoration poets writing of matches played between mixed teams for prizes of cakes, ale and kisses, and often associated with Easter and Shrovetide festivals.

First recorded around 1480, stoolball was one of Britain's earliest organised team games, and probably the first played exclusively by women. If cricket was a game invented by shepherds, stoolball was a sport invented by dairy maids. It was originally played using a milking stool hung from a post or tree as the wicket and a milking bowl as a bat. The name for a milking bowl is a 'bittle' and so the game was sometimes called bittle-battle. Stoolball originated in Sussex (whose inhabitants had a claim on inventing cricket, too) and at one time was so popular there people called it 'the national sport' of the county.

Antiquarian John Aubrey came across a game at Colerne Down in Wiltshire, in 1671 and noted that the players 'smite a ball stuffed very hard with quills and covered with soale leather, with a staffe commonly made of withy, about three and a half feet long'. When Aubrey handled the ball, he found it about 4 inches in diameter and 'hard as stone'.

Aubrey thought the game was played only in the West Country but, in fact, it seems to have been popular across England and Wales. Joseph Strutt, an eighteenth-century antiquarian and engraver from Chelmsford in Essex who was the first great chronicler of English games and sports, tells us that stool-ball (as he styles it) 'is practised to this day in the northern parts of England' but using the hand instead of a bat. The game was so well known by the late eighteenth century that it features in Samuel Johnson's original English dictionary.

The first recorded match was in the 1750s, while the inaugural inter-county match was played between Sussex and Kent in 1797 on Tunbridge Common. To distinguish the two sets of players, the Sussex team wore blue ribbons and Kent pink. The game I was watching at Glynde Recreation Ground was part of a tradition stretching back way beyond that of organised football.

In East Sussex the game had enjoyed a huge surge of popularity in the Victorian era – hence the presence of the *Evening Standard*'s correspondent – and soon many villages had clubs, practised regularly and travelled long distances to play their matches. Parish's *Dictionary of Sussex Dialect* records that the players 'display such perfection of fielding and wicket-keeping as would put most amateur cricketers to shame'.

The modern rules of stoolball were codified in Glynde in 1881. The game is played on a field 90 yards in diameter. The pitch is 16 yards long, the 'wickets' are square pieces of wood attached to a post at shoulder height (in the 1870s, the correspondent of the *Graphic* likened these to 'Trespassers Will Be Prosecuted' signs, which is about right). The ball – which is white, leather and stitched like a tennis ball – comes to the batter on the full as in rounders. Runs are scored the same way as in cricket, by running back and forth or by hitting the ball to the boundary rope for a four, or over it for six.

Glynde Butterflies were one of the greatest names in the game. In the Victorian era, the Butterflies team rose to prominence and became so famous that they were arguably the first female sports stars in Britain. The Butterflies' main rivals were the Firle Blues, the Chailey Grasshoppers, the Waldron Bees and the Selmeston Harvest Bugs. If only clubs had marketing arms in those days, the merchandising from those sobriquets would surely have netted them a fortune in income from soft toys.

Like cricket, stoolball was played by people from all walks of life. The Glynde Butterflies team included the daughters of vicars, farmers, gamekeepers and the clerk of a nearby chalk pit. As in cricket, the skipper was rather posh. Gertrude

Brand was the daughter of Henry Brand, owner of Glynde Place, and great-granddaughter of Georgiana, Duchess of Devonshire.

But Gertrude wasn't selected because of her bloodline alone. She was one of the greatest batters of her era, a point she proved by smashing stoolball's first-ever century, 110 against Chailey Grasshoppers in 1868. Remarkably, the score didn't include a single boundary, which meant a lot of running in a floor-length skirt, bodice and hat. If Brand had been dressed in shorts and a T-shirt, she might well have scored 300.

Gertrude's stoolball career was cut short at the tragically young age of twenty-five, not by injury, but by marriage. Her sister, Maude, soon took over as star of the team before her career too was cruelly terminated by wedlock.

The Brands' main rival was a certain Miss Dabson of Firle Blues who, according to one Victorian account, 'hits such a mighty swipe in the air it is a sight for the gods to see the girls gaping at the ball in the skies'.

Inspired by the deeds of Brand and her fellow Sussex stars, the game spread all over the country. In 1891, the *Morpeth Herald* carried news of a match between the Northumberland villages of Mitford and Netherwitton. Amy Kershaw starred for the home team, who won by an innings. The style of the report suggests the game was no novelty in the north-east and there is no explanation of the rules.

Glynde Butterflies disappeared before the end of the nineteenth century, but were reformed in 2011, largely due to the efforts of Andrew Lusted, who wrote a lovely book on the history of the original club. 'I only got them together for a one-off game,' he says now. 'I thought the match would draw an interested crowd and a captive audience for my book, but then one of the umpires cried off, so I had to stand out in the field all day. I didn't sell any copies at all.'

Today's opponents were Adastra. They were based in Hassocks and had been set up in 1988. The game at Glynde Recreation Ground started at 6.45 p.m. and with the fixture list announcing that sundown would be at 8.25 p.m., it was plainly going to be a squeeze to fit in the regulation fifteen overs per side.

I'd watched old Pathé newsreel footage of stoolball (in Sussex the soft accent saw locals swallow the first 'L' so that stoolball sounded more like 'stooble') played by ladies in long skirts. The underarm bowling had the look of something one of your aunts might have delivered during a game of French cricket in the front garden when you were an infant. Perhaps that was the way things were in the days of restrictive clothing, but at Glynde Recreation Ground the bowlers hurtled to the wicket and flung the ball through the air at head height at dangerous speeds.

The batters' shots in response didn't have the range of cricket. There was a hook and a pull and what looked like a forehand smash in tennis. With the ball coming through at such a height, so quick and from a distance of about 10 yards, batting was plainly a good deal tougher – and potentially more hazardous – than I'd previously imagined. Despite some difficulties, Shirah Mustarde made a gallant 42 and the Butterflies closed their innings on 108-8.

The Sussex Stoolball League had been founded in 1903 and the game got a bump in popularity a couple of decades later thanks to the singular and energetic Major William Wilson Grantham, a stoolball evangelist who marked himself out from the crowd by appearing at matches wearing a traditional Sussex farmer's smock and a top hat made of beaver fur. Grantham's initial success came in promoting stoolball as a game for invalids and older people. Towards the end of the First World War, the game was taken up by wounded and convalescing soldiers, and Grantham sent out dozens of stoolball sets to field hospitals in France and to veterans' hospitals and service depots all over Britain. Put bluntly: a man with one arm could play stoolball, but he could not play cricket or golf. The game was more leisurely, the bowling less dangerous. In 1919, Lord Justice Eady summarised his own fondness for stoolball. 'As one gets older, one appreciates the value of a game old can play as easily as middle-aged.' It was a game 'suitable for those who can no longer enjoy the more strenuous pursuits'.

By 1922, the game was in rude health thanks to Grantham's ceaseless efforts to promote it. Excluding schools, there were more than 150 clubs in Sussex alone. The *Worthing Herald* went so far as to claim that stoolball 'is now on a fair way to becoming as big a national institution as cricket and football'. This, it should be said, is a claim often made for new or emerging sports. In my lifetime I've been assured by PR people that the fastest-growing sports on the planet have been everything from Padel tennis – invented more than fifty years ago by a Mexican millionaire – pickleball, new age kurling and ultimate Frisbee. Back in 2005, Nordic walking was hailed as Britain's fastest-growing sport. Nordic walking was invented in Finland to overcome health problems arising from the traditional northern European diet of lard and beer. It could have been called Lapp jogging, but for some reason they passed that opportunity over.

Grantham, who lived at Balneath a few miles from where I was now standing, founded the Stoolball Association of Great Britain, published books on stoolball that showed how to play the game and organised an annual exhibition match at Lord's cricket ground. This must have taken some efforts of persuasion as up until that point, aside from cricket, Lord's had only staged two other team games – lacrosse (one match in 1876 featured a team of ex-patriot Canadians against a side representing the Iroquois Nation) and baseball (an 1874 encounter between the Boston Red Stockings and Philadelphia Athletic). The baseball game had attracted 5,000 spectators. No records seem to exist of how many people came to watch the stoolball, but the games had a similarly exotic flavour. The seventh match, for instance, played on October 1927, saw Grantham's XI take on the Japanese Embassy. In a bid to spread stoolball across the globe, Grantham's selection had an international aspect, but while Icelander Gisli Karlsson made a respectable three not out, Herr Dr Feine of the German Embassy failed to trouble the scorers. When the

Japanese batted, M. Matsamura notched a decent twenty-eight, but his colleagues could not match him and Grantham's side triumphed by fifty-three runs.

Despite Grantham's strenuous efforts, stoolball never did match the popularity of cricket, let alone football. By the 1940s, the game's popularity around Britain had dipped. In Sussex, however, it still held an important place in the lives of local women and photographs of stoolball teams creating ceremonial arches with their bats to honour a newly wed team-mate were a weekly feature of the local press throughout the 1950s and '60s.

Andrew Lusted thinks claims that the game might have been approaching the status of cricket in the 1920s are a little exaggerated. 'William Wilson Grantham did a good job of promoting the game, particularly in schools. He set up associations all over the country, but after he died during World War Two, they faded away.' Stoolball retreated back to its heartlands: Sussex, Kent, Surrey and Hampshire.

At Glynde Recreation Ground, Adastra's innings had begun and it rapidly became clear that 108 was not a total the Butterflies' bowlers were capable of defending. Becki Denslow slapped a rapid half-century and her team romped home with a third of the overs still remaining. Adastra Ladies would finish second in the table, while Glynde struggled all season. They failed to win a game and finished bottom of the league.

The appeal of stoolball seemed obvious. It was a lot cheaper than cricket. Bats retailed for £50, balls were £7, wickets could be had for £150 a pair and the players didn't need pads or helmets. And, since the ball didn't bounce on its way from bowler to batter, the game could be played on any field. It was fast and exciting, yet like hockey and shinty it had somehow been marginalised. It was hard to fathom why, though equally difficult not to conclude that the fact the game was played mainly by women was a major contributory factor.

Lusted agrees. 'I think the fact it was largely a female game had a lot to do with it. It was always treated seriously in Sussex. The reports in the local newspapers are matter-of-fact. But when journalists came down from London to watch a game, the articles they wrote tend to be lascivious and patronising.' The female players were regarded in rather the same way Samuel Johnson looked upon the woman preacher. 'Like a dog walking on its hind legs, it is not done well, but you are surprised to see it done at all.'

That wasn't such a problem today, but life had moved on. Women were playing cricket and football at high levels, drawing large crowds. Stoolball had remained small. 'I'd say we do OK,' Andrew Lusted says. 'We bobble along.' Which in these uncertain times is something we might all aspire to.

I headed off in search of the Castle Inn, probably the only pub whose beer had been praised as 'the best in the country' by a British prime minister (though since that was Stanley Baldwin, there was a chance that title no longer held).

Lewes had some claim to being the obscure sports capital of Britain. Not only was it a centre for stoolball, but it also hosted the toad-in-the-hole world championships. Toad-in-the-hole is a pub game in which players try to throw small brass discs into a pocket in a table from a distance of about 9 feet. It combines elements of darts, shove ha'penny and snooker. Back in the 1970s, it had looked on the verge of oblivion with only four tables left in the pubs of Sussex. The world championships had revived the sport and now tables were springing up like, well, toadstools in a cow field.

Even more importantly than that (imagine!), Lewes Castle was the site of what may be the last old-school bowling green in the world. The Lewes Castle Bowling Society green is not flat. It is a natural piece of ground as bumpy as the average grassroots football pitch. It also slopes. The green has been used since before the English Civil War, making it one of the UK's oldest sports fields. This is the sort of bowling green Sir Francis Drake may have played on (if indeed he did play bowls at all), and certainly King Charles I and others did. It is said that Tom Paine played bowls here at Lewes shortly before emigrating to America where he was instrumental in bringing about the revolution against British rule.

Despite the important role a bowler played in the formation of their nation, the Americans have surprisingly never embraced the sport, though they did take a fancy to stoolball. The game had been carried across the Atlantic by early English immigrants. The stern-faced old Puritan William Bradford, who arrived in New England on the *Mayflower* in 1620, wrote disapprovingly in his journal on Christmas Day 1621 of seeing men frolicking in the streets of the colony, 'some pitching de barre [a kind of caber toss], some at stoole-ball and such–like games'.

In the form of stoolball we know today, the players run up and down as in cricket, but Joseph Strutt also records a variant in which the batter ran around a circle marked by milking stools. It was this style of stoolball that most baseball histori-ans now believe became America's pastime. William Wilson Grantham may not have achieved his aim, but stoolball had travelled further than most people imagined.

4

Knock Her Head Off, Billy

AUNT SALLY, OXFORDSHIRE

It had been a tough week. First of all, I went to the barbers and when I came to pay, I was told by the young woman who'd cut my hair that the charge was £7.50. This was a surprise to me, as I normally paid £9.50. 'Your prices have gone down,' I said. The young woman looked at me quizzically. 'Oh sorry,' she said. 'Are you not a pensioner, then?' This blow to my self-esteem was nothing compared to the following day when I had my first ever pedicure.

Standing 6 ft 5 means I have a similar relationship to my feet as Britain does with the Falkland Islands: I know they belong to me, but as to what goes on down there I have only the vaguest idea. It was therefore with some feelings of unease that I approached my appointment.

There were other reasons, too. When a man enters late middle-age, he experiences certain physical changes. Some you expect; the fact our stomach no longer looks like an iron-ing board but more like the pile of laundry sitting next to it is hardly a revelation. Others come as much more of a surprise.

Recently a friend of mine went to the doctors because he thought he had some rare form of tinnitus, only to be informed by his GP that the 'weird rustling sound that seemed to follow him everywhere' was the hair in his ears.

I was in no position to laugh, having just discovered a hair growing out of one of my earlobes that was so thick you could have used it to fish for pike and so long I could have fashioned a Bobby Charlton-style scrape-over hairdo with it.

I knew something weird was going on a year ago when the lady who cuts my hair said, 'Would you like me to trim your eyebrows?' And then, after a pause, she added helpfully, 'I won't sculpt them. I'll just cut off the wiry bits.'

Worst of all, though, is what seems to have happened to my toenails. They are now the colour of nicotine and as thick as the shell of a giant tortoise. Add to that the fact that the skin looks like rhino hide and, in the immortal words of Jerry from *Parks and Recreation*, 'I've a corn on my right toe so big it should come with butter on it.' You will have gauged that my feet are not a pretty picture. In fact, even Francis Bacon might have rejected them as too startling to be rendered for public view.

So it was with some trepidation that I removed my shoes and socks and revealed the contents to the pedicurist. Politely, she did not pass comment and the next hour went by with relatively little incident. 'Why do you do that thing with the cuticle – push it back and trim it?' I asked her once my confidence had grown. 'Oh, a lot of people find it gets snagged on their tights,' the pedicurist replied.

I told her I didn't often have that problem.

Her comment reminded me of a few years back when I was appearing regularly on a Channel 4 sports show. The woman doing the make-up asked if I had any preferences on what shade of blusher she used.

I said I had never really given it any consideration.

'I suppose most men don't,' she said. 'At one time I'd thought there might be room for a range of men's cosmetics, so I designed a few samples. I got my husband to take them to work and see if he could interest his colleagues, but he didn't get anywhere with it.'

'What does he do, your husband?' I asked.

'He's a motorcycle officer with the Metropolitan Police.'

As the pedicure continued, I tried not to watch too closely, but I did glance down when she was cutting my left big toe nail and saw that she had both hands on the clippers and was gritting her teeth like someone trying to get the rusted cap off an oil can. I tipped generously.

As if this head-on collision with the ageing process hadn't been bad enough, I was now travelling to Oxford on the Megabus. Travelling on the Megabus was a bit like moving back in with your parents – nobody did it because they wanted to. Unfortunately, the cost of a train ticket from Newcastle to Oxford was exactly £37 more than I'd recently paid for a return flight to Bologna on British Airways, so here I was, less through choice than as a means of ensuring my entire bank balance wasn't shifted into the grasping hands of Avanti.

The Megabus was actually quite comfortable compared to the old National Express buses, or at least it would have been but for a woman four rows behind me, talking into her phone in a strident estuarine voice set at a pitch that would make dogs howl and pigeons fly into windows. She was speaking to a work colleague and if you'd been playing a drinking game in which you sank a shot of Jägermeister every time she uttered a cliché of modern management-speak, you'd have passed out by the time we reached Chester-le-Street. Which, on balance, would have been no bad thing.

'We don't have the bandwidth for a nationwide B2B roll-out,' she said. 'You need to upcycle the optics on these verticals ... drill down ... turbo-boost our brand aware-ness ...' At some point she fell silent, possibly because the person on the other end of the line had interrupted her to say, 'If you're so bloody great, how come you're on the bloody Megabus, then?'

I put on headphones and watched out of the window as we rumbled through a landscape of truck stops, junctions, service stations, block motels and overpasses on which lone middle-aged men in anoraks leaned against the parapet, star-ing at the flowing traffic like a heron surveying a river for fish. Occasionally, a forlorn-looking stretch of countryside would peep out, only to be swallowed up by a drive-through burger bar offering a jumbo chai latte. On we went through Shudehill Interchange, Navigation Street and Coventry Pool

Meadow bus station – places that, I must reluctantly confess, are by no means as glamorous as they sound.

Nine hours after setting off, I had my reward – the village green at Marsh Baldon in Oxfordshire. The vast expanse of grass, said to be the biggest green in Europe, stretched for hundreds of yards in front of the Seven Stars pub towards a row of thatched cottages that were nudging towards the punchable end of cute. A couple of dog walkers were standing chatting. They were holding their ball-throwers at waist height, which gave them the look of priapic Satyrs from a Greek play.

The Seven Stars is a place of some sporting renown, since it lays claim to having been the place where Aunt Sally was born as a competitive, organised sport. It was also home turf for one of the greatest of the game's 'sixer-men', a chap named Greenaway who topped the scoring charts in the Oxford & District Association year after year in the 1960s. The pub had once had a fine display of trophies and relics from the early days of Aunt Sally, but new owners had taken the place upmarket, and though there was still an Aunt Sally pitch tucked away at one end of the garden, the Seven Stars' great days at the forefront of the game were now in the past.

To watch a game being played I travelled over to the Fleur de Lys pub in East Hagbourne near Didcot. The Fleur de Lys played in the forty-eight-team Abingdon and District League. This was far smaller than the original Aunt Sally league, the Oxford & District Association, which boasted 120 sides spread over twelve divisions and involved some

1,400 players. But, even so, it was a considerable number of teams and players for a game that few outside Oxfordshire had even heard of.

The Fleur de Lys was a splendid white-washed seventeenth-century pub across the lane from a half-timbered thatched cottage that looked like it earned a living modelling for the lids of chocolate boxes. I went into the bar and ordered a pint of Morland bitter because that seemed the sort of thing Inspector Morse would have been drinking if he'd come here (and since it was in the CAMRA Guide, he surely must have done) and wandered off to find the garden.

I had seen some of the players arriving carrying their sticks in what looked like carpenters' bags. I knew they took good care of them, sanding them regularly and dusting them with talc so they didn't stick. It seemed like I was in for an entertaining evening and then something happened that I hadn't anticipated – it poured down, great drops of rain the size of budgerigars. The players went out and came back in again. The sky darkened to the colour of pond mud. Some of the team members hung around smoking and vaping and muttering. It wasn't a fit night out for sheep, never mind two pub sides. Eventually they went back indoors and so did I.

The rules of Aunt Sally are mercifully short – almost literally written on the back of a postcard, judging by the old set issued by the association in Oxford. The object of the game is to throw a stick and knock over the target, known as the doll. The doll looks like the sort of thing that might top a bedpost or the end of a curtain rail. It is painted white and stands on top of a black metal pole about 30 inches high. Behind the doll is a sheet of canvas or tarpaulin on which is painted a large black spot to make the doll more visible.

A judge stands off to one side. His or her job is a tricky one. In Aunt Sally you score a point for knocking over the doll, but your shot is invalidated if it hits the iron pole first. Since the sticks hurled at the doll are the size of rolling pins and whirl through the air, it's the sort of judgement that is hard to call. VAR might at last be useful here, but thankfully nobody has any time for it and the decision of the judge is final.

The distance from the wooden throwing strip (known as the 'hocking' or the 'hockey', like the oche in darts) to the target is 30 feet. Each team has eight players who throw six sticks each, which comprises a round called a 'horse'. A match is the best of three horses. Strikes are called 'crosses' while a miss is a 'blob'.

Throwing must be underarm, but there are a bewildering variety of techniques. Some favour a style that sends the stick through the air like a javelin, lengthwise. Others opt to launch it with in sidearm style that sends the stick spinning and parallel to the ground. This seems to offer the bigger chance of a strike because it's using the full length of the stick, but it's hard to keep the stick horizontal and if it's wobbling, the chance of striking the pole is greater.

With one point per doll strike and eight players throwing six sticks each, Aunt Sally's equivalent of a maximum break is forty-eight. As far as anyone knows, no team has ever achieved this milestone. The highest team score ever made was forty strikes from forty-eight throws by the Edward VII pub at Hinksey way back in 1962.

The early history of Aunt Sally is uncertain. Some credit its invention, like that of darts, to Royalist soldiers, who evidently spent their time playing games while Cromwell was busy training his cavalry. Since Charles I set up his court in Oxford after fleeing London, this has some resonance. Whoever invented the game, he or she was clearly no animal lover. Aunt Sally was originally played not with a pot doll, but with a live hen. The hen was tied to a pole. Competitors threw sticks at it. Whoever killed it took it home. Most sports in Medieval England involved fighting, killing animals or encouraging animals to kill each other. Popular pub names give the game away. The Fox and Hounds and the Fighting Cocks are fairly obvious, but even the apparently innocent Dog and Duck refers to a once-popular pastime of pinioning ducks' wings and then setting them off across a pond and seeing which dog could catch the most. Don't be too judgmental – this was before the internet. Besides, we might congratulate ourselves that however horrible this pastime, it was nowhere near as obnoxious at the Argentinian sport of pato. In this remarkable contest, teams of South American cowboys galloped about the pampas across pitches several miles in length trying to score a goal with a live waterfowl ('pato' is the Spanish word for 'duck').

Pato was highly hazardous. And not just for ducks. Players were knocked senseless in brutal challenges and the wielding of knives was considered an integral part of the fun. Even in the robust and distinctly uncosseted society of 1700s Latin America, pato was considered far too dangerous to exist. It was frequently banned by the authorities in Buenos Aires and, at one point in the late eighteenth century, Catholic priests refused to offer men who had died playing the game a Christian burial in a bid to put an end to the madness. It proved futile.

Joseph Strutt documents a whole range of sadistic pastimes that range from bear-baiting to 'the spinning of chafers and of butterflies'. For a man born and raised in the Georgian era, Strutt had an enlightened attitude when it came to animal cruelty. He takes a dim view of all baiting and even lambasts the guardians of children he has seen firing pins at flies using a blow-pipe: 'the judgement of that parent must be exceedingly defective, or strangely perverted'. Doubtless many contemporaries harrumphed that he was a liberal do-gooder and muttered, 'You can't even torment a badger these days without the PC police jumping all over you,' but that is the way of human progress.

Strutt writes about horse and dog racing, but one sport involving animals he doesn't mention is pigeon racing. That's because the first race wasn't held in Britain until 1881, eighty years after his death. Pigeon racing had been invented in Belgium roughly thirty years earlier, but quickly spread to England and around the world. It was massively popular in unexpected places such as Taiwan, South Africa and Romania. In Britain, pigeon racing was gradually falling out of favour, with the numbers of racing lofts dropping by around 5 per cent annually. That wasn't fast enough for some people.

The sport, once thought an entirely innocent fun, has lately been denounced as 'utterly cruel'. And not by some woke whippersnapper either, but by armed forces favourite Dame Vera Lynn. It is fair to say that so far the twenty-first century has not been good as far as pigeon racing is concerned. The number of participants has been falling, more and more birds have been getting lost – confused by mobile-phone signals, picked off by falcons ... The explanations vary, though perhaps the most persuasive was aired to me by a veteran birdman a few years back: 'One time when a bird got old, you put it in a pie, but these days the young lads just let them go on indefinitely.' Part of pigeon racing's appeal in tougher times was that it was – like champion vegetable growing – a hobby you could eat. These days people go to Tesco.

Those pigeons that do find their way back home are coming under increased scrutiny. Pigeons are sometimes called 'the racehorses of the skies' but, given their habit of attracting scandal these days, they seem more like the racing cyclists of the clouds.

Doping scandals have proliferated since Belgian police raided lofts in 2001, with the difficulty of drug-testing pigeons – how do you get them to pee into a flask? – exacerbated in the UK by the fact that, until relatively recently, the Royal Pigeon Racing Association had to send samples to South Africa to be tested.

Not that drug use is new to the sport. The hope of finding a winning potion means pigeon racing has never been without quacks. The great Belgian writer Georges Simenon recalled how in the 1920s a chemist in his home city of Liège had perfected a particularly potent pigeon purgative that literally lightened a bird's load during races. Local fanciers used to queue round the block to buy it. Presumably it was less popular with everybody else in Liège, with the possible exception of the laundry firms.

Belgium was where pigeon racing was invented (the sport was once so popular they used to show races on television) and it is well known as the centre for what British enthusiasts tend to refer to as 'continental practices'. This state of affairs was brought to my attention back in the 1990s when a north-east pigeon-fancier of my acquaintance asked if I would pick up some 'stuff for the birds' for him while I was visiting Flanders. He knew a Belgian lad, he explained, who had something that could fix the vexed problem of moulting. The trouble with pigeons, he said, is that they shed their feathers during the prime racing months of the season. The fewer feathers they have, the slower they fly, but if you just give them a little dose of this stuff . . .

I envisaged a scene at the customs desk at Newcastle airport in which packets of anabolics and corticosteroids were laid out in front of me by stern-faced officials, and I was forced to confess that I was acting as mule for a bird. I told the pigeon-fancier I didn't think I could oblige.

Later it crossed my mind that if the bloke really wanted to import illegal pigeon dope, he could get the birds to bring it in themselves. This notion might be dismissed as whimsical were it not for the fact that, in Bosnia a few years ago, prison wardens apprehended a pigeon bringing heroin into a jail near Srebrenica. 'We do not know what to do with the pigeon,' the deputy warden, Josip Pojavnik, said, 'but for the time being it will remain behind bars.'

You might wonder why anybody would bother doping pigeons, but the fact is that even nowadays it is a big-money business. In 2020, a bird named New Kim sold at auction for $1.9 million. The winning bidder was Chinese. Presumably he or she won't be eating that bird either, even if it turns out to be a dud.

To return to the matter at hand, Aunt Sally. Once the prospect of winning Sunday lunch was removed, the game seems to have become a children's pursuit. Or as Strutt puts it, 'upon the abolition of this inhuman custom, the place of living birds was supplied by toys in the form of cocks, with large and heavy stands of lead, at which the boys, on paying of some very trifling sum, were permitted to throw at heretofore.'

What the game was called at that point is hard to discern. The name Aunt Sally was imported from the USA where the game was played at county fairs for prizes. The American form of the game was less cruel than the original, but it still had a nasty edge. Aunt Sally was a Black woman and punters were invited to knock the clay pipe out of her mouth, or simply to smack her head off. Eventually, poor Aunt Sally was replaced with a coconut and people who were forever ranting about political correctness gone mad had a reason to get the green ink out and write a letter to the *Daily Telegraph* denouncing 'cancel culture'.

Aunt Sally was then given a gloss of respectability when it became a fixture of village fetes. The first Aunt Sally league – the Oxford and District Association –was formed in 1938, but the game was already popular enough in Oxfordshire for campaigning local politicians to be photographed playing it at their local in a bid to convince voters that they were down to earth and normal.

Quite what gave Aunt Sally this fresh impetus is hard to fathom, but it may have had something to do with the First World War. A couple of other regionalised traditional sports had also seen an upsurge in popularity in the aftermath of the conflict: stoolball, of course, and bat and trap. Both these games, like Aunt Sally, could be played one-handed, involved little running about and featured no violent physical contact. They were therefore ideal pursuits for disabled former service-men. There must have been a psychological element, too. The carnage of the Western Front had left many people in Britain yearning wistfully for a pastoral idyll, the sort of sun-dappled rural world evoked by the poets Edward Thomas (who died at Arras in 1917) and Edmund Blunden (who survived two years on the Western Front as a junior officer in the Royal Sussex Regiment). Playing Aunt Sally in the garden of a country pub on a warm summer's evening amid the scent of honeysuckle and the throbbing trill of song thrushes must have offered the survivors of the Somme, Ypres and Passchendaele a brief glimpse of a world forever lost to them.

After the formation of that first league, Aunt Sally boomed in Oxfordshire and, by the 1970s, the Oxford and District League featured more than 150 teams. Other leagues had sprung up, too. As well as the Abingdon and District, there were also leagues based around Bampton, Banbury, Bicester, Chipping Norton, Kidlington, Wychwood and Yarnton. These days there are close to 3,000 people playing the game, pretty much all of them in Oxfordshire.

The rain continued to play drum rolls on the pantiles of the Fleur de Lys. I ordered a pint of Wibbly Wobbly Whippet (which I couldn't imagine Inspector Morse thinking, never mind saying out loud) and waited for my taxi. When it arrived, I considered asking the driver if he offered a discount for senior citizens, but thought better of it.

5

Buttocking and Velvet

WRESTLING, CUMBRIA

In Carlisle bus station, a trio of girls with sturdy legs studied TikTok footage on a turquoise smartphone. A boy in grey sweatpants tried to attract their attention by circling round them on his bike doing wheelies. The girls looked up, sneered and went back to the phone. The boy continued to circle undeterred, jerking the front wheel of his bike into the air with a grimace of effort. Perhaps he'd seen one of those lists that pop up pretty much every day on the internet telling young men 'Ten Things Women Secretly Look for in a Guy' and 'Doing wheelies' had unexpectedly been number five on the list, just after 'Ability to burp the national anthem' and narrowly ahead of 'Thick spit'.

At the Warwick-on-Eden Showfield, things were distinctly more bucolic and less sweary. The River Eden wound languidly between spreading trees and the red-stone tower of Carlisle Cathedral rose to the south-west above blowsy expanses of cherry blossom. I shuffled through a cheer-ful summer crowd. In front of me, two doughty-looking Cumbrian ladies in Lavenham jackets talked about the chang-ing face of the nation. The first lady brought up a mutual male acquaintance. 'You ask him how he is and you just get this absolute bloody litany of medical issues. His lungs, his back, his waterworks ... Nobody wants to hear all that nonsense. There was a time when you asked someone how they were, they would just say, "I can't complain" and you moved on. But they're all at it now.' Her friend tutted. 'Yes, the whole lot of them,' she said. 'You know who I blame for it? The bloody Americans.'

The two women disappeared in the direction of some huge Charolais bulls and I wandered off towards the wrestling ring. I was feeling very chipper. I love agricultural shows and this was the first I'd been to in what seemed like three years, likely because it was. To me, agricultural shows are as much a feature of a British summer as anoraks, tailbacks and middle-aged men in comedy aprons burning meat to a cinder while on-lookers fish wasps out of their wine glasses and say, 'Actually, I think I'll stick with Twiglets and potato salad.'

I've been to hundreds over the years, ranging from small village affairs to the sprawling county shows that pull in crowds comparable with that of the FA Cup final. It's hard for most people to imagine, as they pick their way past stalls selling fishing fly pictures, statuettes of cows riding motor-cycles and novelty doormats, past the ferret racing, and the dog show, the pony club fancy dress parade, the marquees of obscure rural societies such as Ladies in Pigs ('a voluntary group for women involved in the pork industry') and the trade stands for Semen World (which in any other context might seem like the world's least appealing theme park), but what you are looking at is something that once did as much to save our nation as Sir Francis Drake, the Duke of Wellington and the Spitfire.

By the end of the eighteenth century, Britain was teetering on the brink of disaster. The Industrial Revolution had brought with it a population explosion. British agriculture could not cope with the increased demand for food. Famine loomed. If it was to be averted, farming must transform itself as rapidly and as radically as manufacturing had done.

A new breed of gentleman agrarians, the likes of Thomas Coke, Lord 'Turnip' Townsend, Earl Spencer and even the monarch himself, George V or 'Farmer George' as he was nicknamed, led the reformation. They brought a restless energy to their task, perfecting selective breeding techniques, crop rotation systems and labour-saving machinery. They formed a network of agricultural societies, gave lectures and demonstrations, and published pamphlets. The trouble was that not enough farmers took any notice of them. Then someone, possibly Thomas Coke, whose public demonstrations of sheep shearing had attracted vast crowds to his estate at Holkham in Norfolk, hit on the idea of a show. Here all the advances would be shown and explained, the superiority of the new methods demonstrated and, to encourage good

practices, prizes would be awarded to the best stock and produce. In this context, best invariably meant biggest. At the
agricultural shows, the oxen were enormous, the ewes huge
and the pigs appeared to have been inflated with a foot-pump.
Vegetables were gigantic: leeks like broadswords, endless
carrots, and string beans you could crochet with. Any passing Frenchman would have been tempted to play pétanque
with the peas.

There's a long-term dispute over whether the first agricultural show was held at Wolsingham in County Durham,
Liverpool or Bath. One thing that is agreed on is that it
was around 1780 and that these three set a trend that spread
quickly across the country. The results were dramatic, British
farming was transformed, the nation saved.

At first the agricultural shows were purely educational, but
as the public appetite for seeing big pigs, chunky sheep and
bulls the size of buses began to wane more and more entertainments had been added. Across Cumbria and Northumberland
this included Cumberland and Westmorland wrestling.

When people think of wrestling, they generally think
of burly men with unlikely names – Giant Haystacks, Big
Daddy, Masambula the African warrior, Johnny Kwango, or
perhaps The Rock and Hulk Hogan. They picture bulging
guts, sunbed tans, baby oil, skimpy trunks and holiday camps.
I don't blame them. When I was ten, my greatest treat was
to be taken to the all-in wrestling at Middlesbrough Town
Hall. I would sit in the dress circle between my grandmother
and her friend, Mrs Gawthorpe, gazing down at the ring

and the pantomime carnage that surrounded it and grinning like a fool.

I was not always so happy in their company. Mrs Gawthorpe's husband had – as my grandad put it – 'taken the easy way out' and died decades earlier. She had two children of her own, but they had emigrated to New Zealand. And, to be honest, you couldn't blame them. Frankly, she was so fearsome she made Lord Sugar at his most irritable look like Myleene Klass perusing an Instagram account devoted to photos of kittens wearing feather bonnets.

The wrestling thankfully cheered up Mrs Gawthorpe to a point where she no longer froze the ground she walked on. She focused her eyes on the ring where Jim 'Cry Baby' Brakes was rubbing his knuckles in the face of ex-New York ballet dancer Ricky Starr. Her face wore a look of grim relish of a sort she usually only sported when discussing her gastric complaints during a family tea.

Down below, girls in tank-tops yelled, old ladies in twin-sets and berets shook their fists, and toffees, coins, Murray Mints and lighted cigarettes flew. Every once in a while, some middle-aged woman emboldened with drink and incensed by repeated illegal shenanigans would leap onto the ring apron and whack Brian 'Goldbelt' Maxine or another such villain with her handbag. It was wild, sweaty, vulgar and massively entertaining. And like everything else I enjoyed – cherryade, sherbet flying saucers, DC comics – my parents fretted that it would have a corrosive effect on my well-being.

My greatest night was seeing the cunningly named Kendo

Nagasaki (Karate Hiroshima doesn't have the same air of menace to it, and Judo Bikini-Atoll is way too poncey-sounding) wrestle early in his career. I was deeply impressed with his entrance in a black cape and helmet, brandishing a samurai sword. 'He's a Japanese warrior,' I told my grandad excitedly when I got back. My grandad had been an amateur boxer and regarded the wrestling in much the same way an aficionado of Wagnerian opera might the music of Michael Bublé. 'Japanese warrior!' he snorted. 'I bet he runs a pie stall on Stockton Market.' My grandad, it turned out, was nearly correct; Kendo (real name Peter Thornley) worked at Jennings, the horsebox-makers in Crewe.

My parents needn't have worried. My passion for grappling wore itself out. My grandmother stopped going to the wrestling at Middlesbrough Town Hall. Soon after she was banned even from watching it on television. The official explanation was that it was bad for her heart. Years later, my mother would reveal the real reason: Granny had taken to yelling so loudly and obscenely whenever Mick McManus appeared on the screen that the woman next door had phoned the police.

I'm not sure what my gran or Mrs Gawthorpe would have made of Cumberland and Westmorland wrestling. It was a good deal quieter than the grappling they were used to, the wrestlers had ordinary names like Joe Robson and Michael Johnson, and nobody got hit over the head by the cornerman's bucket. I think my grandfather would have liked it, though, because – like amateur boxing – it was tough, skilful, dignified and genuine.

Cumberland and Westmorland wrestling is part of the rural summer sporting scene across the far north of England and southern Scotland. The season begins when we all concur that it is really too cold to be what you'd really call spring and ends when everyone agrees it is suspiciously mild for what the calendar assures us is late autumn.

You will encounter C&W wrestling, as it is generally dubbed for brevity's sake, at most agricultural shows in the counties that encompass the North Pennines. That acronym can lead to confusion. Presented with a show programme a few years ago, a friend of mine from Nottingham commented: 'C&W wrestling? What's that, then – Shania Twain with Garth Brooks in a headlock?'

It may not be quite as exciting as that, but C&W has a seductive rhythm and grace. To fans of this ancient martial art, the umpire's cry of 'Hods' will forever conjure memories of a place in which the manly scent of lanolin wafting from the sheep pens mingles with the smoke of burning oil from the chainsaw woodcarving demonstration, and the whistles and yells of the shepherds at the sheepdog trials are muted only by the frantic clunk-and-yelp of children smacking one another with toffee apples.

Cumberland and Westmorland wrestling traces its origins back to the Dark Ages. It was once part of a thriving English grappling scene that also included Cornish wrestling (Abraham Lincoln was an adherent), Lancashire Catch-as-Can, Scottish Backhold, Norfolk wrestling (a collars-and-elbow style in which all holds below the 'thucklebone' were barred and contestants looked to execute a Howard's hank, flying hobby or blackguard's snatch), and Devon Hugg, in which the grapplers wore clogs and kicked one another on the lower legs.

Joseph Strutt tells us that wrestling had once been popular in London but that, from the start of the sixteenth century, had 'became unfashionable and was rarely practised by people of opulence', gradually falling from favour with the general populace of the capital. Maybe so, though in 1669 John Evelyn watched a wrestling match in St James's Park in the company of 'His Majesty and a world of lords' between Men of the North and Men of the West. The prize to the victors was the staggering sum of £1,000. The West Countrymen won it. They were in all likelihood the favourites. According to Strutt, the menfolk of Cornwall and Devon learned to wrestle from an early age and even 'the most untowardly among them' were likely to offer the visitor 'a trial of this exercise' whether they asked for one or not – which seems a better way of discouraging tourists than just scowling at them when they enter the pub. As a result of their training, Strutt believed the West Country wrestlers were so good 'that if the Olympian games were now in fashion they would come away with victory'.

The sport's long roots in Cumbria could be traceable back to a 'giant youth' named Gilpin, who was better known locally and nationally as 'The Cork Lad of Kentmere'. Gilpin was the son of an itinerant woman and an evidently not entirely committed monk from Furness Abbey. He grew up dining on porridge and sunlight in a hovel near Troutbeck. Sometime around 1550, the Cork Lad walked to London and, in front of King Edward VI, threw the royal wrestling champion clean out of the ring. As a reward, the king granted him land in Cumberland and the money to build a house, which Gilpin seems to have managed almost unaided – at one point apparently lifting into place a 30-foot-long oak beam single-handedly.

'The Cork Lad of Kentmere' had many gigantic successors, including the Herculean John Woodall of Gosforth in West Cumberland and Launcelot Harrison, a gravedigger from the village of Greystoke who was so huge it was claimed his jawbone was 'half as big again as that of a stout six-foot man'. Given his birthplace, it's hard not to conclude that Harrison may have been Tarzan's grandfather.

The deeds of the great C&W wrestlers of the eighteenth and nineteenth centuries are detailed in books such as William Litt's *Wrestliana*, which tell of the exploits of grappling legends such as Robert Atkinson, the 'Sleagill Giant', who, judging by his cart-lifting exploits, seems to have been Georgian England's answer to the Incredible Hulk, and the splendid 'Miller Robin' Dodd from Brough who, it was said, could lift a 160lb sack of wheat and toss it over his shoulder *with his teeth*. It was a skill that must have come in very useful when he had both hands busy with his knitting.

The obsession with the stature and girth of these wrestlers mirrored the Georgian fascination with the size of livestock. The age of the Sleagill Giant was also that of the Ketton Ox and the Craven Heifer, huge cattle who toured the country to wonder and acclaim.

Wrestling wasn't just about size and strength, however. One of the greatest wrestlers of the Georgian era, Jemmy Fawcett, a miner from Nenthead up in the North Pennines, stood barely 5 ft 7 and weighed a smidge over 10 stone. Yet he won the Melmerby Rounds seven times on the trot starting in 1793, defeating men who often outweighed him by 6 stone. According to accounts, Fawcett was 'as active as an eel and as difficult to hold'. Wriggling and twisting, he threw his giant opponents to the ground in a manner worthy of a martial arts master – but then that, in a way, was what he was.

Another celebrated wrestler was Abraham Brown, a clergyman based at Egremont who'd attended Bampton Grammar School near Penrith (the village of Bampton is also – top fact alert – home to the telephone box that features in the film *Withnail & I*). Brown was the very epitome of the sort of muscular Christianity being pushed by Victorian patriarchs such as Matthew Arnold. During his days as a parson, Brown would happily engage anyone who pitched up wanting to take him on, and by all accounts never lost any of these challenges. He was good humoured, amusing and, 'though occasionally addicted to the bottle', esteemed by everybody in Cumbria.

The Church had not always looked on wrestling so favourably, I should add. The Puritans took against the sport and in a big way. In a proclamation of 1656, the Ministers of Cumberland and Westmorland thundered that 'these counties of Cumberland and Westmorland have been hitherto as a Proverb and by-word in respect of ignorance and profaneness; Men were ready to say of them as of the Jews of Nazareth, can any good come out of them?' Wrestling was, as far as they were concerned, at the heart of depravity.

I took a seat on the grass and watched the opening bout between two teenage lads in shorts and T-shirts. A couple of decades ago, the Cumberland Wrestling Association had repealed the rule that made wearing the traditional costume of velvet trunks, long johns and an embroidered singlet compulsory. The *Daily Mail* claimed this was a case of 'political correctness gone mad', but when I phoned the secretary for an update, he explained calmly that it was just a way of allowing more people to take part. 'Not every teenage boy has a pair of velvet pants in his bedroom cupboard,' he said. It was hard to argue with that.

The teenage boys gave way to a couple of older blokes, one a burly farmer with straw-coloured hair and skin burnished to the colour of tomato soup, the other a smaller wiry man who moved on his toes like a fox terrier.

The bigger man might have seemed to have the advantage, but that wasn't guaranteed. The previous week I'd had an illuminating discussion on this very topic with the man who comes to empty the septic tank. When I phoned him on the Monday, he said he'd be round next day, but he couldn't give a time. He didn't need to, of course, because it is a truth known to all country folk that the septic tank man always arrives when you are eating. This would not be so bad were it not for the fact that he insists on providing a running commentary on operations through the window. 'Very, very solid in your pipes,' he bellows. 'I'm going to have to pump some liquid in to loosen it. Aye, there's your problem – caked tissues and faecal matter.' It was Mrs Gawthorpe all over again.

After I'd thrown my lunch in the bin, I went out to talk to him and spare the neighbours. The septic tank man is about five foot eight and so broad he's practically cubic. He could wear a tea chest as a waistcoat. He comes from up near Hawick and has the sort of crushed face that makes him look like he's got a stocking mask on. He got to look this way playing as a front-row forward in the Borders. The septic tank man's passion for rugby union is proof that the game is not played exclusively by the middle classes. If there's a job less bourgeois than sucking human excrement up from a hole in the ground, then frankly I don't want to hear about it.

The septic tank man said that, in his playing days, the great joy of the return trip from an away match came when the captain spotted a field of cattle. 'We'd get the coach driver to pull over and then we'd get in that field and have a competition to see who could topple a bullock the quickest,' he said with a chuckle. 'It's not all about strength, you know?' he added, in case I'd mistaken late-night roadside cow-wrestling for something unsophisticated and brutish. 'There was a scrum-half who farmed out in Teviotdale. He couldn't have weighed more than nine stone, but he could have a stirk on its back in five seconds flat. Pure technique, that was.'

Cumberland and Westmorland wrestling was a rural pursuit. Many of the men who entered were farmers with experience of grappling livestock. Sure enough, the smaller man in the ring in front of me now had the better knowledge of holds, leverage and angles, and took down his bigger foe with a gracious ease.

Tom Harrington from Carlisle was refereeing. He nodded with approval. Aficionados recall Harrington as one of the greatest wrestlers of his generation. Not only did he win an MBE for his services to the sport, but one of his elaborately decorated wrestling outfits was exhibited in the Tate gallery. I saw him fight towards the end of his career. He had grey hair by then and wore wire-rimmed spectacles. When he took off his glasses to wrestle, they left red marks on the bridge of his nose that gave his pale face a look of vulnerability. Below the neck, he was as thin as a foxhound with muscles that bulged like knots in steel cable. When he took on younger, less experienced men, he was surprisingly mild, not so much throwing them to the ground as setting them down with a gentle flourish, as a faithful retainer might a well-stuffed picnic hamper.

The number of wrestlers entering competitions like the one at the Cumberland County show was no longer what it once was, which was why the rules on costumes had been relaxed. Nor was the sport ever again likely to attract the sort of crowds that had once packed into the Agricultural Hall in Islington to watch London's annual Cumberland and Westmorland wrestling event. In the Edwardian age, 3,000 people had paid to watch that show.

Yet there were grounds for optimism. C&W was no archetypal local sport, of interest only to local people. Its governing body remains part of the International Federation of Celtic Wrestling (or *Fédération Internationale des Luttes Celtiques* to give it its proper name), which holds an annual world championships – a kind of grappling equivalent of WOMAD – and draws entrants from Iceland, Hungary, northern Spain, Friesland and Gran Canaria. In recent years, traditional wrestlers from Britain have travelled to belt-wrestling championships in Istanbul and Kazakhstan, while every now and again the local scene in Northumberland has been enlivened by the arrival of a troupe from Brittany. The Bretons wrestle in their traditional garb of three-quarter-length trousers and white vests decorated with the Gwenn ha Du, the black-and-white Breton flag. When not in action, they cluster at the side of the ring, proudly wearing the dark silk sashes of their club and shouting out encouragement and tactical advice to their compatriots. This is something of a departure from the normal way of things. Traditionally the spectators sit in an intense contemplative silence, broken by ripples of applause for a well-executed cross-buttock, and a spontaneous outburst of feminine cooing whenever a dark-haired Scot known as Clark of Milngavie strips down to his long-johns, embroidered vest and velvet trunks. There's clearly something about the sight of a man with his drawers on over his tights that excites a woman. Perhaps the lad at the bus station might give that a go after he's abandoned the wheelies.

6

The Crack of Steel on Bone

SHIN-KICKING, GLOUCESTERSHIRE

A soldier, writer and intimate of Charles I, Sir John Suckling was a tall and handsome man of reckless bravado. When he pondered his place in history, the swaggering cavalier likely hoped to be remembered for his racy love poems, or perhaps a gallant deed on the battlefield. It was not to be. Suckling's poetry is a literary footnote, his military career a pratfall. Sir John, however, did achieve immortality of a sort. His memory is invoked whenever we use the phrases 'level-pegging', 'left in the lurch' or 'streets ahead', or speak of being 'bilked' in a deal. Because, shortly after he was knighted in 1631, Sir John Suckling invented the card game cribbage, and it's cribbage from which those expressions come.

These days cribbage is considered a fusty old relation of bridge and poker, a game played in pubs by elderly men such as *The Archers'* Bert Fry, who died (literally 'pegged out') after a game in The Bull in 2021. It was not always so, however. Sir John Suckling was a gallivanting playboy. According to John Aubrey, he won more than £20,000 (about £4 million today) playing cribbage with marked cards. True to form, he quickly lost it all. Destitute and in exile in France after a hapless attempt to spring the Earl of Stafford from the Tower of London, Sir John – Aubrey records – took 'poyson, which killed him miserably with vomiting'.

While other seventeenth-century card games such as Bone Ace, Queen Nazareen and French Ruff faded into obscurity, cribbage became ever more popular with people from high society to low. The game is portrayed in the satirical sketches of Thomas Rowlandson and crops up in the novels of Anthony Trollope, Rudyard Kipling and Daphne du Maurier, though undoubtedly the writer who did most to bolster cribbage's popularity was quoits-playing novelist Charles Dickens. The great Victorian writer was an expert cribbage player himself and the game features in *Oliver Twist*, *The Mystery of Edwin Drood* and most notably in *The Old Curiosity Shop*, in which the whimsical eccentric Richard Swiveller teaches it to the raggedy little girl he names the Marchioness.

Sir John's invention has few rules, but endless subtleties and permutations. The objective is to be first to score the target number of points (usually sixty-one or 121) by playing card combinations. The points are marked on the cribbage board using pegs. The rows of holes – grouped in fives – are known as streets, hence 'streets ahead' and 'level-pegging'. The area behind the start line is 'the lurch', so if you are so comprehensively beaten and your pegs are still there when your opponent 'pegs out', you are 'left in the lurch'. Bilking is a form of cheating.

By the start of the twentieth century, cribbage was Britain's national card game, such an integral part of life that when new licensing laws proscribing gaming in pubs were introduced in 1968, cribbage was not included. It remains the only card game you can play for money in a British pub without the landlord requiring a special licence.

Now, Sir John Suckling had a friend – a fellow poet, card-player and gadabout. His name was Robert Dover. Dover was pretty much the Baron Pierre de Coubertin of the seventeenth century, and he was the main reason I was now standing on the side of a hill in Gloucestershire watching two young men kicking each other's legs.

Dover was born in Norfolk in 1580, attended Cambridge University and then studied law at Gray's Inn. After qualifying as a lawyer, he moved to Gloucestershire, settling in Saintbury with his wife, Sibilla. Thanks to his charisma, charm and the fact that he had acquired a set of King James I's cast-off clothing – which gave him a distinctly fashionable, not to say regal air; Strutt says that Dover wore the king's clothing 'with much more dignity in his air and aspect' than James himself – Dover quickly found favour with local big cheese Sir Baptist Hicks. A cloth merchant, Hicks had been knighted by King James shortly after loaning the Crown a vast sum of cash. Doubtless this was a coincidence.

Through his fancy connections, Dover ended up in charge

of Chipping Camden's annual Whitsuntide gathering. By 1612, the event had been moved out of the town and onto the place where I was now standing: Kingcombe Plain, or, as it is known today, Dover's Hill.

Dover had a classical education and a poetical concept of the bucolic life. Worried that the traditional innocent fun of the English countryside was in danger of being obliterated by the Puritans, he set about preserving the idealised Merry England of contemporary poets and playwrights – a world of capering rustics who spent summer evenings drinking cider, dancing, romancing and – at times – playing stoolball.

The man whose clothes Dover paraded around in, James I, had recently issued his *Book of Sports*, which listed all permissible pastimes – archery, dancing, leaping, vaulting – alongside those which were evidently to the detriment of the common good. The latter included bull-baiting, bear-baiting and, of course, that most unruly and savage of all games, lawn bowls.

On Kingcombe Plain, Dover's Olimpicks featured only those sports that were permitted by His Majesty. According to Joseph Strutt, the games consisted of wrestling, cudgel-play, leaping, pitching the bar (an English version of tossing the caber), throwing the sledge hammer, tossing the pike and hare coursing. There was also gymnastics and, inevitably, morris dancing. King James had an inexplicable passion for men in bowler hats jinking about hitting each other with inflated pigs' bladders, but then since he also kept a flock of hunting cormorants in a purpose-built brickhouse in Westminster, perhaps that is not so surprising.

By the 1630s, the Cotswold Olimpicks were well known around England and drew curious spectators from as far afield as London. Among them were Prince Rupert of the Rhine and Dover's pal Endymion Porter, who, as well as having a name that sounds like a craft beer, was also an art collector, diplomat and future groom of the royal bedchamber.

Then, in 1642, the English Civil War began. The Olimpicks carried on for a couple of years, but were cancelled in 1644. A year later, royal benefactor Sir Baptist Hicks' great house Campden Hall was burned down by troops loyal to King Charles I. Dover died in 1650 and the games seemed to have been interred with him. There was no room for frivolity in the England of Oliver Cromwell. Unless you got a jolly thrill out of burning Levellers alive, obviously.

The Restoration brought the fun and frolics back into English life. Charles II liked to be entertained. When he called in at the annual sports day at Bodmin in Cornwall, while on what seems to have been a very circuitous route to Sicily, he enjoyed himself so much he became 'a brother of the jovial society' that ran it.

While no one appears exactly certain when Dover's games returned, they seem to have been well established again by the early 1700s. With Britain's puritanical streak apparently sated for a while, all restraints were off. The Cotswold Olimpicks plunged downmarket. As well as brutal cudgel fights, the games also included running races for young, and scantily clad, women. The winners of events picked up prizes in the form of gloves, hats and smocks. Naturally these events drew a large crowd of what are traditionally described as 'curious onlookers', presumably because 'they can't really be bothered with it onlookers' and had better things to do with their time.

The Cotswold Olimpicks continued in this raucous vein for the next hundred years, with various sports added and taken away. By the end of the Napoleonic Wars, the games featured wrestling, horse races, sack races and a version of blind man's bluff that was called 'jingling' because those running away wore bells on their ankles. By now, cash prizes were being offered by sponsors (usually local pubs) alongside the usual belts, items of clothing and the occasional canteen of cutlery.

The railways increased attendances at the games, which in the 1850s had risen to 30,000. The rising crowds also brought the showmen with their exhibits, cons and hucksterism. I have a bitter recollection from my own childhood of a booth at Stokesley Fair named the House of Wonders. This was the last vestige of the old freak show exhibits that had once been one of the mainstays of touring fairs. Over the centuries these garish sideshows had featured everything from Miss Hipson 'The Middlesex Wonder – Fattest Child In All The Kingdom' to an oyster that apparently smoked a pipe. There was also 'The Giant Congolese Negress', who was actually Victorian showman par excellence David Prince Miller dusted with soot and sporting a grass skirt and a well-stuffed brassiere. It may not seem like much of a disguise, but it was good enough – or so Miller claimed in his autobiography – for him to have received numerous marriage proposals from a variety of gentlemen.

The House of Wonders was misnamed on two counts. Firstly, it was not a house but a tent, and, secondly, the only thing of wonder about it was that people would willingly pay money to enter it. Friends who did spend their pocket-money emerged grossly disillusioned with the cunning and perfidy of mankind. The Siamese twins were plasticine, the two-headed calf was pickled and the three-legged chicken was, one reported memorably, 'just a normal hen with a wooden leg stuffed up its bum'.

Even that was better than what went on at some fairs, though. A decade ago, I met a very elderly gentleman who recalled as a schoolboy in the 1920s queuing for an exhibit at Marlborough Fair that promised, 'She wears nothing but a smile!'

'People went in through the front of the tent and exited through the back,' he explained. 'Very clever, you see? I was waiting half an hour, my anticipation rising by the moment. A naked lady! In those days, even the sight of a woman's knee was a cause of huge excitement. I imagined a mermaid, a lady from the harem of the Sultan of Turkey. I paid my sixpence, went in and you know what? "She" was a bloomin' sheep!'

'And was the sheep smiling?' I asked.

'To be honest,' the old gent said, 'I was too disappointed even to notice.'

The old gent had taken his lesson calmly, if glumly. Others didn't react quite so well to being conned. Outbreaks of violence, fighting and rioting often ensued.

Across Britain there was a tide of moral outrage about the behaviour of 'the mob' at events. Prize-fights and horse racing had seen spectacular violence, while the old pleasure fairs frequently ended in mass brawls. The Olimpicks were no different with violence no longer confined to the cudgel, wrestling and shin-kicking rings.

By the 1850s, the games had become, according to one writer, 'the trysting place of all the lowest scum of Birmingham and Oxford'. As is common with other areas of hooliganism, outsiders were blamed, in this case usually 'roughs from the Black Country' or the Irish navvies who were building the nearby Mickleton Tunnel.

Like the pleasure fairs, the Olimpicks became the target of the same Victorian moralists who trimmed the Cooper's Hill wake. In 1862, it was held for what to many seemed like the last time. By the 1870s, it was being written off as if it was ancient history, a half-remembered relic of a more licentious and unruly era.

England had not lost its Olympics entirely, however. The Much Wenlock Olympics had begun in 1850, the brainchild of a local doctor, William Penny Brookes. While Dover's Olimpicks had risen from the boozy wildness of the traditional country fairs, the games in Shropshire were a very different beast. The Wenlock Olympics were again part of the Victorian drive to create a nation of healthy Christians. The games included an odd assortment of competitions that over the years included quoits, a donkey derby, a 'sprint for old women' and a penny-farthing race. In the 1920s, when interest had begun to wane, circus acts (including a duo of 'Funny Chinese Laundrymen') were invited to perform. Yet despite all that, and the fact that cash prizes – alongside clocks and sets of fish knives (perhaps, like in *The Generation Game*, they should have thrown in a cuddly toy and a foot spa) – were awarded to winners, the ethos behind them was much more akin to the Corinthian notions of Baron Pierre de Coubertin than Dover's version. Indeed, it was a visit to Wenlock that set the little Frenchman on his path to creating the first modern Olympics. For all their quirkiness and village carnival atmosphere, the Wenlock Games were a respectable part of the sporting establishment.

Dover's Olimpicks languished for several decades. A revival of interest in rural activities sparked by the Arts & Crafts movement – of which Chipping Campden was an important centre – saw the Cotswold games again coming back into focus. A campaign led to Dover's Hill being bought by the National Trust in 1929.

The Olimpicks finally made a comeback as part of the Festival of Britain in 1951. The games that year included a pageant featuring a local man dressed as Robert Dover and a host of new sports: boxing, obstacle races, a donkey derby and pillow fights. One ancient sport that was revived was the shin-kicking. A crowd of more than 2,000 people watched the final between a chemist's assistant, Joe Chamberlayne, and local farmer, Ben Hopkins. Both contestants wore steel toe-capped hobnail boots. The bout was said to have been 'punctuated by loud groans from the contestants' and lasted for nine minutes, at which point Chamberlayne landed 'a deft right foot kick above Hopkins' ankle' and felled him.

An attempt to hold the games annually was scuppered the following year by an outbreak of foot-and-mouth disease. Enthusiasm flickered and dimmed, with the Whitsuntide celebrations on Dover's Hill confined to bonfires and morris dancing. But, in 1965, members of the Scuttlebrook Wake Committee grouped together and founded the Robert Dover's Games Society. They staged their first games the following June under the name Robert Dover's Cotswold Olimpicks. The games have taken place regularly, if sporadically, ever since (foot and mouth, a lack of funds in 2017 and, inevitably, COVID-19 had all led to cancellations). Events changed over the years. There had once been motor-bike scrambles, piano-smashing, poetry and professional all-in wrestling. One thing remained constant, however, to prevent a return to mob rule: alcohol was banned, though judging by the smell of some of the people around me, a lot of folk had brought their own supply.

That afternoon, the games had begun with the arrival on horseback of men dressed as Dover and his friend Endymion Porter, to the accompaniment of a military band. It was early evening. Swallows skimmed over the toy-like wooden fort, an imitation of the 'castle of boards' described by Joseph Strutt, though small cannon were no longer 'frequently discharged' from its battlements, more's the pity. The sports area was fenced off and a temporary stage stood to the right of the fort. Spread out before me, the Gloucestershire countryside was a luscious and perfect rendition of what many non-British people imagine England looks like. The scenery had such higgledy-piggledy quaintness it might have been created by the anime team from Studio Ghibli after reading *Cider with Rosie.*

Several thousand people had assembled and seemed affected by the same benign mood. We were entertained by a dance troupe, a race across an obstacle course, a display of old-school stick fighting carried out by two men dressed in black and wearing masks that called to mind my old hero, 1970s grappler Kendo Nagasaki. There was also a standing long jump contest. The latter had once been an event at the modern Olympics and was dominated by an American, Ray Ewry, known as 'The Human Frog'. Ewry's best jump was a barely credible 3.47 metres. Nobody came close to matching that on Dover's Hill, which is hardly surprising, since Ewry's 1904 leap is still a world record.

Time ticked on and, as the light began to fade, I felt a certain tension in the air. Things were building towards the event that traditionally headlined Dover's Olimpiks, the shin-kicking championship.

It has to be said that this is by no means as brutal as it once was. Shin-kicking had evolved from Cotswold wrestling, a traditional style much like the Cumberland and Westmorland version. However, such was the ferocious animosity between the local villagers that they soon stopped trying to trip each other and commenced hoofing one another instead. The

NO PIE, NO PRIEST

new sport of shin-kicking soon became a popular event at wakes and fairs across Gloucestershire and neighbouring Worcestershire. According to a report in the *Sunday Mercury* in 1936, 'competitors wore heavily nailed boots with metal tips projecting. Oftentimes these tips ran to a point,' which suggests that the rustic shin-kickers of the West Country might have inspired Ian Fleming's SMERSH supervillain Rosa Klebb.

Competitors began to toughen their shins by pickling them with vinegar (a trick perhaps borrowed from conker players) or desensitising their legs by beating them with coal hammers. Some took to increasing the sting their kicks inflicted by coating their toe caps in acid extracted from the gall bladders of sheep. Others adopted even more elaborate methods to tilt a contest in their favour. In a bout at Pershore Fair in the late 1800s, the 'short but well-proportioned' Champion of Bredon took on a man known simply as 'The Chipping Camden Giant'. The Giant towered over his opponent by a head. Despite this apparent disadvantage, the Bredon champ triumphed. It was later revealed that the toes of his over-sized boots were filled with lead, adding weight and power to his kicks, as well as making it more difficult to knock him over.

The results of these ruses were not pretty, but seldom fatal. The *Sunday Mercury* related the tale of parish constable William Payne, a champion shin-kicker whose legs looked like a relief map of Gloucestershire and yet who lived to the ripe old age of ninety-one.

Still, there was enough gore to alarm the authorities. The 1850 event at Dover's Hill was particularly brutal. J. Wilson of Lark Stoke took on A. Wilson of Broadway. The contest ended with one of the Wilsons – it is unclear which – writhing on the ground in agony having suffered a broken leg. Alerted to the goings-on, local justices intervened. Denouncing shin-kicking as a barbarous pursuit, they ordered the sport stopped, doubtless to much head-shaking and mutterings about 'how the bloody world's gone bloody soft' in the pubs of Chipping Campden, Ashton-sub-Edge and environs.

As if to further irritate the sort of common-sense folk who are forever saying things like, 'These days they call it a coma, in my day they called it bone-idleness', the organisers of the Cotswold games have outlawed heavy boots. Training shoes are now worn, but the basics remain the same. Two competitors in front of me, each dressed in farmers' smocks, had straw stuck up their trouser legs and bound in place with gaffer tape. They seized each other by the shoulders and when the referee (known as the stickler) called, 'Go!' they began kicking each other between ankles and knees. In shin-kicking, as in most wrestling, the first man to hit the ground is the loser. The bouts were generally over pretty fast, though a couple did go on for five minutes or more. Whether that was because the contestants were evenly matched, timid or plastered it was hard for the first-time watcher to tell.

The event was a straight knockout, the final held as the sun began to sink over a landscape so calm and lovely if it could have spoken it would have sounded like Joanna Lumley. Even the knowledge that, somewhere out there among the undulating greenery, David Cameron was sitting in a shepherd's hut smirking could not spoil it.

7

Thunderous Dairy

CHEESE ROLLING, GLOUCESTERSHIRE

I attempted to see the Cooper's Hill cheese-rolling three times. The second time it was cancelled due to the foot and mouth epidemic of 2001 that resulted in the culling of six million sheep and cattle, the third time by COVID. Since, in 2022, Russia had just invaded Ukraine and estate agents had taken to publishing maps showing the places in the UK where your property was least likely to be struck by a nuclear warhead, I took the selfless decision not to make a fourth try for fear that my arrival in the Cotswolds would precipitate Armageddon.

On the first time I tried to see the cheese-rolling, in 1998, I actually got as far as the hill only to find the entire event was teetering on the verge of oblivion. I called round at the house of retired engineer Tony Peasley, of the Cooper's Hill Cheese-Rolling Committee, to find him fielding telephone calls from TV companies in Australia and Francophone Canada, and radio stations in Japan and the Netherlands. 'The minute we announced it was off, the phone started ringing,' Peasley said. 'It's international news.'

The cheese-rolling, held near Brockworth on the western edge of the Cotswolds, is one of a family of bizarre ancient customs spread across the nation, a close relation of the Helston Furry Dance, second cousin to West Witton's Burning the Bartle, maternal aunt to the Hallaton Bottle Kicking.

These events are often portrayed as some cuddly subsection of theme-park Britain, or as a self-reverential celebration of national eccentricity. The savage, pre-Christian undertones of some, and the knuckle-sandwich element of others, preclude such fluffiness.

When I mentioned the cheese-rolling to a cab driver in Gloucester, he said that it was 'carnage up there, absolute bloody carnage', with the mixture of delight and disapproval that so often characterises men speaking of violence.

This was an aspect of the event which, given recent health and safety concerns, the organisers are understandably keen to play down. 'Far too much has been made of that side of things,' Tony Peasley told me. 'It's all got grossly exaggerated.'

When I spoke to cheese-rolling aficionado/comedian Andy Smart, he took full responsibility for the situation. 'Back in 1995, I was writing pieces for *Maxim* about weird events and I did a piece on the Cooper's Hill cheese-rolling.' Incredible though it is to believe, in those days *Maxim* was selling more than 100,000 copies a month. The cheese-rolling evidently struck a chord with the readership. 'The following year about 4,000 people turned up to watch. There were stag parties and everything. That was what caused all the problems. Before that, it had been under the radar. I've always felt very regretful about that.'

Tony Peasley had arrived in Gloucestershire from South Wales in the 1950s. He moved into cheese-rolling and married into it, too – his father-in-law was on the cheese-rolling committee. In the forty years he'd been involved in the event, Peasley insisted that nobody had ever been seriously hurt. 'The sort of injuries we get are cuts, abrasions, dislocations and sometimes the odd concussion,' he said.

The St John's Ambulance Brigade that provides the medical cover adds breaks and fractures to the more painful end of Peasley's list.

Whatever the truth, the taxi-driver's view persists. On the day of the cancelled event, at the foot of the slope down which an 8-pound Double Gloucester cheese bounces like a Barnes-Wallace dam-busting bomb pursued by a galumphing herd of runners of various levels of fitness and inebriation, two young men in designer T-shirts sat in a Fiesta XR2 and scowled at the hand-painted sign announcing the cancellation. 'You'd have thought some 'ardcore cheese-rollers would have turned up and done it anyway,' one of them said in a West Country accent with sufficient rasp to rip the hair off a coconut. 'We come all the way from Bristol hoping to see some severed limbs and that, didn't we?'

I had thought a lot of the health and safety talk was baloney until I stood at the bottom of Cooper's Hill. Looking up at it gave me the same vertiginous feeling I'd had ten years earlier standing below the ski-jump in Garmisch. 'It's not so much a hill as a cliff,' Andy Smart says, and he's not far wrong.

Smart says that he was only foolish enough to actually compete in the cheese-rolling once. 'That was in 1997. It had been a very hot summer and the ground was rock hard. About seventy people entered and there were thirty-three injuries – three broken collar bones, broken wrists and ankles, a couple of blokes knocked each other unconscious in a collision – it was mayhem. They had to hold the second race back by an hour while they waited for the ambulances. I was at the back so I saw it all happening. I slid down on my backside most of the way.'

Smart has not given it a second go. 'I've run with the bulls sixty-two times in Pamplona and across the rest of northern Spain, I've played in the Ashbourne football match half-a-dozen times and gone down Ben Nevis on a lilo, but the Cooper's Hill cheese-rolling – once was enough.'

The danger to competitors and to the increasingly large crowds that come to watch the headlong plunge were the core arguments of those campaigning to have the cheese-rolling abolished. Provoked, according to the committee, by inflammatory articles in the local press, Gloucestershire County Council, which owns the land on which the event takes place, had become increasingly fearful of public liability law-suits. ('Had an accident that wasn't your fault?' 'Yes, it occurred while I was innocently pursuing a large orange cheese down a steep incline . . .')

Meanwhile, the police had become concerned about the problems of controlling a crowd that – thanks to Smart – numbered more than 4,000, most of whom arrived in cars. The parking was a nightmare, the nay-sayers complained. The single-lane track up to the hill, and to the dozen or so houses that clung to the side of it, was blocked. The emergency services couldn't get in or out. What if there was a fire? Or a terrorist attack?

The committee might have resisted the pressure. They had already moved the start from its traditional 6 p.m. to 2 p.m. to limit the crowds and the drinking. But when they failed to secure the services of the cave rescue team, they reluctantly cancelled the event six days before it was due to be run.

To the columnists and leader-writers in the right-wing press, this was viewed as a further indication of the Nanny State and the health and safety brigade's attempts to turn us into a nation of cowardly, cossetted weaklings. In truth, bureaucratic interference in British folk customs is almost as old a national tradition as Cooper's Hill cheese-rolling itself. This was not the first time the event had fallen foul of the authorities. Originally it had been the finale of an annual wake or fair held on the brow of the hill. It was the blue-riband event in a day of races, sports and games that also included 'grinning for the cake', 'jumping the bag' and 'chattering for a bladder of snuff' (the latter open only to 'old women').

By Victorian times, there was growing concern about the unruliness at public gatherings such as the Cooper's Hill wake. In 1871, to deal with the menace, Parliament passed the Fairs Act, which allowed local magistrates to abolish any fair, wake or annual event they felt was the cause of 'grievous pubic immorality'.

The wake on Cooper's Hill did not long survive after that. What grievous immorality went on is not recorded, though doubtless the lure of a bladder of snuff may have led to some salty altercations between the elderly ladies of Brockworth, Bentham and Cranham.

According to Peasley, no one knows when the rolling of cheese down a 1-in-2 gradient began. Some say it was a pagan welcome to spring created by Baal-worshipping Phoenician traders (who, to be fair, seem to take responsibility for just about anything odd that goes on the West Country). More likely it began in the late eighteenth century as a means of preserving common grazing rights at a time when the Enclosures Acts were transferring six million acres of communal land into private hands.

Though it has been moved from Whitsuntide to the Spring Bank Holiday, and is no longer preceded by the raising of a new pole for the weathervane that pokes from the top of the hill, the ritual has otherwise altered very little. A master of ceremonies in a white smock decorated with lily of the valley and cornflowers, and a silk top hat adorned with red, white and blue ribbons, calls for volunteers from the crowd. A field of between twelve and forty runners is assembled. The MC begins his count. On three, the cheese is released, on four the runners set off in tumbling pursuit. They have no chance of catching the bounding truckle, which reaches speeds of 80mph as it bumps down the tussocky hill, but the first runner to arrive at the bottom collects it as a prize. These days, five races are run – three for men and two for women.

Since the 1980s, fell runners started to travel from Cumbria in pursuit of the cheese and other competitors arrived from Kent, Shropshire and beyond. There is little chance to train or practise. There is a cheese-rolling event at Randwick near Stroud, which forms part of the local Wap (the revival of an ancient fair featuring, amongst other things, an official Mop-Man tasked with cleaning the streets and the crowd), but it is a tame occasion compared to Cooper's Hill. The only comparable event in Britain used to take place at Uffington in Oxfordshire, at the end of the annual scouring of the white horse, when a cheese was rolled down the bank known as Horse's Manger. But no cheese has been rolled at Uffington since the First World War. Cooper's Hill stands alone.

The Double Gloucester used at Cooper's Hill was made by Mrs Smart of Churcham – no relation to Andy Smart – who uses the milk from a mixed herd of Holsteins, Brown Swiss and local Gloucester cattle. The latter always looked to me a benign kind of a beast, with the amiable face of an auntie offering a plate of scones to a venerable priest. When I mentioned this to Mrs Smart, however, she snorted at my naivety and told me she had recently had her Gloucesters de-horned after one of them gored her in the milking parlour.

The rolling cheese has cardboard discs placed on either side of it and is firmly bound with coloured ribbons. During the Second World War, when food rationing prevented the use of a whole cheese, a wooden substitute was made with a symbolic sliver of cheese inserted in a hole in the middle of it.

Since Hitler could not prevent the Cooper's Hill cheese-rolling, it was certain that local councillors wouldn't either. At 6 p.m. on Bank Holiday Monday 1998, Peasley and his fellow committee members held a quiet and rather solemn cheese-rolling, the pursuing pack made up of just four schoolchildren. Hours later, you could still see the tracks left in the grass, though which had been made by feet and bottoms and which by a runaway cheese, only an expert could have judged.

Thanks to my selfless decision not to try to see it, the Cooper's Hill cheese-rolling of 2022 went ahead as planned. 'It was great,' Andy Smart says. 'An American student who was Inter-railing round Europe heard about the cheese-rolling, turned up the day before, entered and won the women's race.'

There was also yet another triumph for cheese-rolling's answer to Sporty Payne – Chris Anderson. An ex-serviceman, Anderson has won twenty-three cheeses during an undefeated career. 'He's amazing,' Andy says. 'He keeps retiring and then coming back.' In other sports, Anderson's peerless talents might have earned him a fortune, but not in cheese-rolling. Back in the 1990s, when he first began competing, the winner took home the Double Gloucester, while the second-placed runner got a postal order for £5 and the bronze medallist a postal order for £3.

'He claims the secret is to drink six pints of cider first, so you are loose and relaxed. He does this thing where he tucks himself up, rolls and then springs up again. He's an absolute genius.'

8

Metal Melody

QUOITS: NORTH YORKSHIRE AND NORTHUMBERLAND

It was spring half-term and I was waiting at Middlesbrough station among a mighty scrum of day-trippers heading for Whitby. F. Scott Fitzgerald once wrote that 'a ride on a train can be a terrible, heavy-hearted or comic thing'. A prescient observation from a man who had never encountered an Avanti buffet car, yet one from which there is plainly something missing. For despite the savage pruning of Britain's branch lines by Dr Beeching and his followers, there are still train journeys in England that offer more than potential hilarity or nervous dread. If the author of *The Great Gatsby* had ever ridden on the Esk Valley line, he would surely have slipped a 'joyful' in there as well. This, after all, was the train trip that moved his compatriot, the notoriously snarky Paul Theroux, to Edward Thomas-like lyricism. Theroux was correct, too. On the right day, in the right weather, the trip on the two-carriage train from Middlesbrough to Whitby can indeed seem like 'the highest stage of civilisation'. And it rises even a notch above that when you are heading to Egton Bridge to watch a match in the North Yorkshire Quoits League.

While the word 'miraculous' is thrown around in football and other sports, quoits can rightfully claim to be the only game with an actually honest-to-God, Vatican-certified miracle attached to it. The wonder took place in Salisbury in 1409. Richard Wodewell, a carpenter, was playing a game at a local inn when one of his steel quoits struck a nine-year-old girl on the head. She dropped to the ground apparently dead. Filled with horror and remorse, Wodewell sought divine intervention and carried the girl's body into Salisbury Cathedral, laid her down near the tomb of Bishop Osmund and prayed over her. Shortly afterwards, she sprang back to life. Osmund was subsequently sanctified following an investigation by the Papal Commission. It would be nice to think that, in light of the events which led to his canonisation, Osmund had become the patron saint of the badly aimed, but sadly that seems not to be the case (he prefers to devote his powers to toothaches and ruptures).

Quoits was said to have been introduced into England by Roman legionaries. By 1361, the sport was so widespread among his soldiery that Edward III ordered it banned as an unwelcome distraction from more martial pursuits. Henry V also tried to put a stop to quoiting, fearing its popularity would detain Englishmen from practising their archery.

In Georgian Britain the quoit was often used as a synonym for the Ancient Greek discus. The fact the same writers
also refer to the javelin as a 'dart' created the impression
that the goings on at Mount Olympus resembled that of an
English public house, with Zeus at the oche seeking a double
19 to finish, while Poseidon was out at the front trying to
land a ringer.

In the nineteenth century, quoits was played by a greater
number of people in Britain than cricket. Cribbage-fiend
Charles Dickens enjoyed games when rambling around
the home counties and there are reports of games being
played everywhere from Plymouth to Aberdeen. Big-money
matches with stakes of £50 per side were commonplace with
large crowds paying sixpence a piece to watch matches such as
the one between John Rae and William Stewart at Bruntsfield
Links in Edinburgh in 1883.

In June 1870, the *Sportsman* reported that a great crowd
had gathered at Holland's Royal Woolwich Gardens – a
pleasure ground after the style of Vauxhall Gardens with
regular attractions including Lupino's Comic Ballet Troupe,
Tiny Tim, 'The Phenomena in a Smock Frock' and Nix the
Demon Dwarf – to watch a championship match between
George Graham of Sunderland and Robert Walkinshaw of
Peeblesshire played for £100 per side. The two men were both
in their mid-thirties and had been in training for the event,
the Englishman at Woolwich and the Scot at Alexandria near
Dumbarton. History seemed to favour the Scotsman who
had defeated Graham the previous year at McLaugh's Quoits

Ground in Glasgow. Walkinshaw had not lost a match for eight years and in that time was said to have picked up £870 in prize money at a time when a bank clerk earned around £1 a week. The match, which was on an 18-yard pitch, lasted for two days and was played over 120 'heads'. On the final afternoon, the underdog Graham emerged victorious by twelve points.

The first quoits international had taken place in 1896. England faced Wales at Cheltenham – most likely at Beaufort Cricket Field, the home of Cheltenham quoits club – in 1896. George Graham, victor of Woolwich Gardens, was on hand for the English alongside another celebrated player, Sergeant Balfour of Reading. The Welsh stars included Williams Price and Herbert from the coal mining town of Brynmawr. England ran out winners by 308 points to 209. They would carry on playing international matches until the 1930s, but then gave up. Wales and Scotland, however, continued meeting once a year and in the twenty-first century, an English team made up of East Anglian players finally rejoined the fray.

From the Great War onwards, for reasons no one can quite explain, quoits began to give ground to other sports – darts, billiards, bowls – until by the start of the new millennium it was confined to just a few tiny and isolated pockets of the country: Dyfed in Wales, Suffolk, the North Riding of Yorkshire, Teesside (home to Darlington Quoits Club, Britain's oldest, organisers of an annual world championship) and Northumberland where it is centred in three distinct areas around Tweedmouth, Bedlington and the Tyne and Allen Valleys.

Packed and noisy, the eastbound train slid out of Middlesbrough station and off through Gypsy Lane (a place that, like Brambles Farm and Daisy Hill, proves that the lovelier and more romantic a place name, the grimmer the reality) and out into the suburbs of Marton and Nunthorpe (a middle-class enclave of such louche reputation that for years the word 'naughty' was traditionally appended to the front of it by everybody on Teesside. Except those who lived in Nunthorpe, obviously.) Then past the village of Great Ayton, where I grew up, and the conical Roseberry Topping, a mini-Matterhorn that is such a beacon to returning natives that even thinking of it makes Teesside tough guys snuffle.

The carriages were jammed with day-trippers and holiday-makers bound for the coast. There were families with B&B bookings, their suitcases stowed in the luggage racks and net bags bulging with beach games hooked over seats, whose relatives had come to wave them off as if they were bound for some distant and inaccessible shore. And there were OAPs in beanie hats, canvas holdalls stuffed with knitting and malt loaf cradled on their laps. Among this chattering, colourful mob there was a pale goth couple with matching purple nail varnish and nose rings. They were going to Whitby not for the phenomenal fish and chips, the mini golf on West Cliff, or the tea dance at the Pavilion, but because it was where Dracula came ashore in the shape of a large black dog and proceeded to inflict his singular blend of insomniac erotic terror on various local women. While everyone else hopes for sunshine, the goths perhaps long for one of those North Sea frets that cloak the harbour in pale cold mist, so that the ruined clifftop abbey seems to hover like an island above cloud and the calling of the gulls in St Mary's churchyard echoes like the maniacal laughter of tormented souls. This, at least, is what I imagine; they may just want a Mr Whippy ice cream and a go on the waterfall of pennies like the rest of us.

At Battersby, among hanging baskets and African marigolds, what was the front of the train becomes the back. The driver hops out of his cab and saunters down the platform. Passengers keen to face in the direction of travel switch seats with a clatter of buckets, spades and cricket bats. Ten minutes later, the train sets off again. Kildale is nestled in woods, the steep hillside's softly merging colours unfurl like a roll of tweed. At Castleton. I look down on a cricket field through a fringe of dog roses. At Danby – spiritual home of Yorkshire Quoits - there are mauve-and-white acanthus spears and pointillistic balls of midges hovering over the slow, green River Esk.

I got off the train at Egton Bridge and strolled down the main street, past gardens filled with lupins. Giant orange ornamental thistle heads waved above a sea of red valerian. I hopped across the stepping stones over the tinkling Esk to the Horseshoe Hotel.

Egton Bridge is best known for its annual gooseberry show. Great Ayton is 20 miles or so to the west of Egton Bridge. To us, the annual gooseberry show, held since 1800, had a legendary quality. The fathers of many of my schoolmates had gooseberry bushes in their gardens or allotments (after all, how else would Yorkshire babies have been made?) but while their berries might turn up – stewed, in crumbles, or as jam – on tea tables around the village, the thought of entering the Egton Bridge show would have sent a shudder down the spines of even the most confident local gardener.

The growers of the Egton Bridge Gooseberry Society – the Harrisons, Harlands, Ventresses and Welfords – had a fearsome reputation. Their pruning techniques had been refined over centuries, their powerful plant feed – a mix of horticulture and alchemy – made fruit swell like juicing body builders. They were as dedicated as monks. It was rumoured that, in the days leading up to the show, the Egton growers sat out among the bushes shielding their fruit from the sunshine with umbrellas to prevent it over-ripening and bursting. No wonder they were invincible. Every August it seemed a world record tumbled. Even the maiden category (not for unmarried ladies, but for those growers who had never won a major prize) attracted berries the size of pullets' eggs. The thought of striding proudly into the famous exhibition room in St Hedda's Primary School, only to return home broken and humiliated, deterred all but the bravest exhibitor. No man wants people sniggering at his gooseberries.

Egton Bridge is still a place of world beaters. In 2020, Graeme Watson's champion fruit went straight into the *Guinness Book of Records*, but Britain is less insular, people less fearful. These days, exhibitors turn up from across the North

Riding and from as far afield as East Anglia. A few years ago, a party of gooseberry fanatics travelled to Eskdale from Sweden.

Back in Victorian times, when gooseberry shows were common across the north, there'd been a lot of hoopla surrounding the Egton Bridge show – additional attractions, coconut shies, merry-go-rounds and the like – but in the twentieth century it had been pared back to its simple essence. Inside the hall were long trestle tables covered with pristine white cloths upon which the star attractions were perched on bottle tops in fours, pairs or singles, opulent jewels of fruit in shades ranging from creamy yellow to deep red. The biggest of them was the size of a golf ball. Around the walls, wooden plaques carried the names of the winners stretching back through the centuries. The exhibits were weighed on the famous Egton Bridge scales, oil-damped and twin-panned. The judges had first used troy ounces, but now employed the avoirdupois system of grains and drams. The rules of the Egton Bridge Gooseberry Society are simple – the berry must have an unbroken skin and, well, that's it.

Both competitive fruit growing and quoits were summer pursuits. They were pursued by the villagers of my childhood with equal zeal. To emerge victorious at either was to become a local celebrity, the sort of man or woman people would see enter the pub and nudge their companion, give them the eyes and mumble, 'You know who that is, don't you?' To me, gooseberries and quoits are as intermingled as the scent of bracken and heather blowing off the moor tops.

*

At The Horseshoe, I met up with an old schoolmate of mine, Bob, who farms in Bilsdale, one of the skiff-shaped valleys that run into Eskdale. Bob speaks with the slow, wheezing accent of the North Yorkshire Moors, every elongated vowel like the sound of a plump man sinking into a favourite leather armchair. In common with most people from the area, his delivery is so understated, so deadpan, he makes Buster Keaton look like Jim Carrey. 'See that road?' he said, pointing across the dale after we'd exchanged pleasantries. The road ran diagonally down the steep hillside, the merging colours of which gave it the appearance of a rather snappy plaid. Near the bottom it was ambushed and engulfed by hedgerows that were splattered by foam-white elderflower and creamy cow parsley. 'I was stood out here a little before you arrived and a couple of cyclists come down there,' my friend said. 'There were talking to one another and I could hear every word clear as a bell. I thought to myself, *I bet there's not many places in England so quiet that you can listen in on a conversation that's going on over a mile away.* It's a really marvellous place, is this.' Bob paused for a moment to let the thought sink in. 'And now I suppose it'll piss down.'

I told him I'd been coming to the Esk Valley for more than fifty years and not much had changed in that time. Bob thought for a few moments and then said, 'There's a new bridge over by Glaisdale.'

Bob had been playing quoits for many years, though in what he regarded as the superior Danby Invitation Quoits League. He'd played regularly against one of the legends of the game, Paul Dixon from Sneaton. Dixon had won the annual Northern Quoits Association 'world championship' singles eleven times between 1998 and 2019, as well as the prestigious Wilkinson's Sword at Darlington Quoits Club's North of England Invitation Quoits Championships also on eleven occasions. 'The word genius is overused,' Bob said, 'but . . .'

Bob had been lured into quoits from the pools team. Reluctant at first, he'd become such a convert that he'd built a pitch behind one of his barns so he could practise. Bob says that at least he was discreet about this. There is a legend of another local player who installed a pitch on his front lawn while his wife was away in Lanzarote with her sister. 'She went mad when she saw it, apparently,' Bob says. 'He had to build her a conservatory, or he'd still be kipping in the spare room.'

The game we were watching today between Egton Bridge and Fryup (possibly the most evocatively named village in England) was, I'd once assumed, what quoits looked like everywhere. The rules used here had been agreed in the 1880s after the formation in Stockton-on-Tees of the Association of Amateur Quoits Clubs of the North of England. The association published its rules in the *Field* in 1881. This provoked a storm of protest from quoiters around Britain who were playing the game quite differently and who made it very plain they intended to continue to do so no matter what a load of jumped-up busybodies in the north had to say about it.

The North of England rules set the throwing distance as

11 yards and the weight of the quoits at 5 1/4 lbs. They also stated that the pins (called hobs) were set in beds of 'tempered clay' and that the hob should project no more than 3 inches above the surface.

In Scotland and Wales, this produced derisive laughter. To the Celtic quoiters, the northern English game sounded like something fit only for children, ladies and the sort of blokes who favoured patent-leather pumps and pomade. In Scotland, they threw quoits that weighed over 10lbs a distance of 21 yards – as if to prove that the English were a big bunch of milksops. In Wales, they threw the same mighty quoits, but only 18 yards – as if to show that there was a suspicious degree of over-compensation going on in Caledonia (in 1955 the Scots finally abandoned the extra 3 yards and fell in with the Welsh).

Despite the proud stance of the Scots and Welsh, and the fact that for most of Britain clay-end quoits remained a northern mystery, the long game has struggled to keep going. In Wales, there are just eight clubs remaining, mainly in the sort of isolated villages in which clay-end quoits is played, while in Scotland there are only three clubs, scattered around the country – Prestwick, Renfrewshire and Aberdeenshire. Blame for the decline in popularity generally falls on the continued rise of football and the closure of the coalmines, though both factors might equally be cited in Durham and Northumberland.

The long game survives in England only in Suffolk and north Essex, where a handful of clubs still exist. The game had been banned in East Anglia for a sizeable chunk of the seventeenth century. This was because the region was a hotbed (though frosty-bed would be more accurate) of Puritanism and the home of Oliver Cromwell, who generally took a dim view of pretty much anything that didn't involving praying, fighting or scourging heretics. In fact, if the Suffolk quoits players had thought things through properly, they'd simply have replaced the hobs with Quakers. The sight of the steel rings thrumming off the craniums of members of the Society of Friends would surely have earned them a thumbs-up from the Great Protector instead of a jail term.

Having warded off the Puritans, quoits bounced back in East Anglia; by the 1750s, the game was probably as popular there as anywhere in England. Joseph Strutt came from Essex and was particularly biased towards quoits, which he described as an amusement 'superior to any of the foregoing pastimes ... because this exercise does not depend so much upon strength as upon superior skill'. Since the East Anglian game required players to hurl an 8lb quoit 18 yards, Strutt's claim that the sport doesn't require physical strength suggests the author was a chap who could chuck a lump of metal weighing the same as a family-sized frozen chicken the length of a badminton court with the same ease with which most of us could flick a pea across a dining table.

The game continued to flourish in East Anglia in the nineteenth century, but thereafter went into a sharp decline. Tim Finn lays the blame on the fact the game is distinctly muddy – but if that were the case, plenty of other games, such as rugby union, would surely have fallen by the wayside. More likely it was because, unlike in the north, no leagues of any size were ever founded. Without the sharp edge of competition and raucous local rivalries, no sport can really thrive.

In 1980, the Association of Amateur Quoits Clubs of Northern England became the much-easier-to-acronymise National Quoits Association. Despite its name, the NQA still only covers the north-eastern part of England. As well as the Esk Valley, there are also leagues in south and north Northumberland, Swaledale, Arkengarthdale, Teesside and in the southern half of County Durham.

The game between Egton Bridge and Fryup began with the clatter, chink and slap that I remembered from my boyhood. The game is simple, up to a point. There are six players to a team. Each player has two quoits and is paired with an opponent. The players throw two quoits each from one end, take the score, then move down and throw from the other. To the idle observer, it would seem that the only point of the game is to land the quoit over the pin, a shot called a ringer, which earns two points. However, since the only ringer that scores is the one that finishes on top, good players tend only to go for it if they are shooting last – to avoid a dead ringer. The first aim of most players is defensive, landing a quoit so that its edge overhangs the pin, preventing an easy ringer. This can be counteracted by throwing quoits that land on the lip and flip it over. As I say, only the top ringer scores, except if both ringers belong to the same player; this combination earns quoits' single highest score of four. Singles matches are played to eleven points and doubles to twenty-one. The teams score one point per winning game and the team with the most points is the winner. There, I told you it was simple.

Like all sports, quoits has its own language. The outer sloping ring of the quoit is called the 'hill', the inner is the 'hole' or 'face'. The quoit can be gripped in various ways, hill or hole side up or down, on the left or right. Each hold has its name – there are push pots, hill gaters, Frenchmen and housekeepers.

Opinion differs as to how best to throw a quoit. In the Esk Valley, they tend to throw underarm from the right side of the body after a short run up of two or three paces. In Northumberland, they usually throw backhanded from a slight crouch, imparting spin on the quoit which, perhaps like rifling in a gun barrel, helps it follow a more accurate line. The quoit travels through the air with flight and dip. Watching it reminds you of an old-fashioned spin bowler. 'When I started out,' my friend says, 'the skipper of the team, he was a right fanatic, mind, used to draw me diagrams of the different angles of flight. He'd stand watching you at practice going, "Ooh no, lad, she's wobbling like a ruddy duck."'

Some of the old men sitting around us seem like they'd say something similar. Gathered at pitchside, they offer wisdom and wisecracks from mouths that rarely seemed to open wider than is necessary to sip bitter or suck on a cigarette.

There is little messing about in quoits. A game lasts for a couple of hours, but that's only because the teams get on with it. The players fling their two quoits quickly and without apparent ceremony. When they land flat on the clay, the quoits make a wet slap like a palm striking flesh. When they strike each other, they clang and sparks fly. The players move from end to end with business-like rapidity, tea towels tucked in their waistbands chef-style to wipe the clay off the quoits.

The clay ends are the game's distinct features. When not in use, they are covered over with large, heavy wooden hatches to stop them drying out, giving the impression to the uninitiated passer-by of sunken beehives. The clay is smoothed so that it slopes away from the pin, preventing moisture from gathering. Preparing the clay is an art in itself – too hard and the quoits will bounce out, too soft and they will be easily dislodged. 'You're wanting your quoit to stick, not go belly up,' my mate Bob says with some relish.

'That's ow-er!' an Egton player calls as his partner's quoit lands angled over the pin, like a slipped halo. A debate ensues. Players surround the end, feet apart, knees bent, hands resting on thighs, studying the position of quoits. 'You have to have a clear view of the pin through it,' one player announces. The match referee is called the trig man, which may be short for trigonometry. He steps in and takes a look. 'There's some clubs,' Bob says, 'where they'll have him measuring which is nearest by slipping a ten-pound note between the quoits and the pin.' There's no need for that here. The trig man makes his decision. The players nod. The game moves on.

A few weeks after the Egton Bridge match, I watched a game of quoits at the Wallace Arms in Featherstone. The Wallace

Warriors played in Division Two of the Allen Valley Quoits League, which had been formed in 1988. 'There were other leagues before that, but way back,' says league secretary Richard Macdonald.

When it was founded, the Allen Valley League comprised just six teams. Now there are twenty-four, spread over three divisions. Over the past ten years or so, new quoits pits have been installed at half a dozen pubs and also at Corbridge Cricket Club. 'The game's in pretty good health,' Richard says with commendable understatement.

Quoits was traditionally associated with mining. There were coalpits in several of the villages that have teams in the league – Bardon Mill and Acomb, for instance. In the hills of the East and West Allen there was mining too, for lead and tin. The village of Allenheads was once the biggest producer of lead on the planet – a Pennine equivalent of a goldrush town without the get-rich-quick potential but with added poisoning. The metal is mined out now and the coalpits have gone. The game here, as in the Esk Valley, is a largely rural pursuit, rooted in agriculture. The season runs from April to September and one of the few valid reasons a team can give for cancelling a game with less than twenty-four hours' notice is 'hay time'.

In 1900, Wynn, Timmins and Co. of Birmingham were advertising quoits in local newspapers all over Britain. The quoits were 'hard, bright, wrought steel, bearing the maker's name' and were to be had from all good ironmongers. Those who fancied a go but were uncertain quite how to play could write to Wynn, Timmins and would receive by return a pamphlet detailing 'The rules of this healthy game'.

Quoits was healthy up to a point, though at times, particularly when drink and betting were involved, it could get a little dangerous. In 1786, in a pub yard in Charlotte Street in Nottingham, a 'journeyman framesmith' who was stooping over near the pin was – deliberately it seems – struck on the head by a quoit flung in his direction and lay unconscious for six days. A year later in Oldham, in two separate incidents in the same week, one man was killed and another badly injured after being hit by quoits. In 1798, in Northampton, Job Norton, a member of the Kettering Yeomanry, had his skull fractured by an overthrown quoit and died the next day, while at the Red Lion at Wisbech, a child running across the yard in which a quoits match was being played was struck and killed. The thrower was convicted of manslaughter.

Nowadays, quoits is not by any stretch of the imagination a dangerous game, but midges are certainly one of its greatest hazards. In Northumberland, as in Eskdale, the players carry their equipment in the sort of clip-shut plastic cases that power tools come in. Alongside the quoits plenty of space is taken up with insect repellent, antihistamines and bite treatments.

Before the start of the match, spectators burn paper in a vain attempt to drive the midges off. By the midway point, they have damp bar towels draped on their heads or mosquito nets pulled over faces. Only a brave man or woman wears a short-sleeved shirt at a quoits match.

In football, the place that's used as a byword for harsh and typically British conditions is Scunthorpe. 'Nobody relishes a trip to Scunthorpe in February,' the TV pundits will say, or 'The Spanish lad is playing well at the minute. But let's see how he gets on when it's lashing down in Scunthorpe.'

In the Allen Valley Quoits League, Garrigill fills a similar role. The rattling wind, the furious rain and the swirling fog in that high North Pennine village is legendary, while the midges that lurk in the oak tree overhanging the quoits pitch are the stuff of legend. My father once worked with two Texans who'd spent spells on the North Slope oilfields in Alaska. 'It was so cold in the winter, when you farted it came out as ice cubes,' one of them told him. 'And in the summer there were mosquitoes. Sons of a bitch were so big you could slice a piece off them when they flew by and fry it like a steak.' It seems the midges at Garrigill were of similarly menacing proportions. The George and Dragon has been closed for several years now, a fact lamented by the local drinkers but evidently not by opposing quoits players.

Aside from the midges, the biggest hindrance to match play these days is finding a decent pair of quoits. Each player has his or her own pair, and though they are not marked in any formal way, the participants can recognise their own. Plaintive pleas for quoits occasionally appear in the local newspapers, or on the Allen Valley League's message board. The one company that makes stainless steel quoits is down on Teesside and they will only produce a batch when they have a sufficient number of orders. At £70 a pair, players are understandably reluctant to commit to bulk buying. 'When I first started out, I used to borrow them,' my friend Bob told me. 'I used to ask everywhere for them. Eventually this lad in Ugthorpe says he can get me some. Six months later, he finally turns up with a pair. I stumped up. When I got them home, I noticed they were odd ones. One weighed four ounces more than the other. I said, "Y'bugger."'

In 1954, the *Renfrewshire Gazette* reported that the Houston family who ran Johnstone Ford Ltd were closing down. That was the last firm in Scotland making quoits commercially. At the steelworks in Darlington where my father worked, the apprentices were often set the task of making quoits if a request came in from the town's illustrious quoits club. When my daughter's boyfriend worked at the foundry in the Tyne Valley that casts Anthony Gormley's sculptures, some of the older men there could recall making quoits for players in the Allen Valley League. One of them told him, 'If I'm walking past a game, I can always tell if they are using a set of mine. They have a distinctive sound they make when they strike. There's a music to them.' I had no idea if that were true, but it was a romantic idea for this loveliest of games.

9

Never Bet on Anything That Talks

HANDICAP SPRINTING, SCOTTISH BORDERS

I travelled on the train to Carlisle in a slightly jaded state. Two nights before, my sleep had been disturbed by what I had come to think of as a monstrous hound.

The foxhound was standing in the entrance to my drive when I came home from a friend's house. She was hot and tired and bewildered. The local hunt had run a hound trail that afternoon and she had plainly got lost. Hound trailing was a big sport in Cumbria, the Anglo-Scottish Borders and Ireland (drag hunting – which contrary to myth didn't involve members of the Young Farmers' Club dressed as Bavarian barmaids – used the same principles but with bloodhounds). Hound trailing had started back in the eighteenth century and attracted heavy betting. The Hound Trailing Association had been founded in 1906 and oversaw close to a dozen competitions every week from April until the end of October. There was an annual championship for 'Senior Hounds' and 'Open Pups'. The hounds lolloped at high speed, tongues flailing, over the fells and moors following a track scented with paraffin and oil of aniseed. In the comics I'd read as a kid, dogs were attracted by bags of aniseed balls as surely as ostriches were by the prospect of swallowing an alarm clock, so it was nice to know that at least one of those details was true.

Perhaps the hound in my garden was more a Liquorice Allsorts type of dog but, whatever the reason, here she was. It was around the hour that was once known as 'closing time' and, since there was a fair chance of pub traffic passing by on the road outside, I thought the safest thing for the dog was to bring her into my garden, shut the gate and phone the local hunt to come and collect her.

The trouble was that a garden fence is not much obstacle to a rangy hound that spends its working life leaping over walls. The minute the gate was shut, the dog sidled up to it and hopped over with the ease of a deer. I went out and brought her in again, and the sequence was repeated. After three rounds, I decided to revise my plans. I would bring the dog into the house, shut the door and *then* phone the hunt.

If you ever find yourself in a similar situation, I would advise against this course of action. She was a charming and obedient animal, but like most foxhounds, she was as far removed from a domestic dog as Wolverine is from your average human. The minute I ushered her into the kitchen, all hell broke loose. Within a split second, she was standing on top of the cooker with her nose stuck in a casserole dish. Ushered down from there, she landed briefly on the floor before jumping onto the dining table and running the full length of it, apparently sent tripping on the exotic scent of bananas.

At this point my own dog, a smaller breed of French hunting hound, came scampering into the room. He had been alerted no doubt by the *smell*. Because it has to be said that, in matters of personal grooming, the foxhound was far from ladylike, a fact she confirmed when she finally clattered down from the table and relieved herself in such a voluminous manner I thought I might need sandbags to save the sitting room carpet.

My dog is normally inquisitive to the point of obsessiveness, but at the sight of the foxhound on the table, he turned tail and ran away. Had he possessed opposable thumbs, I believe he would have locked himself in the bathroom. As it was, I later found him peeping from behind the sofa like a first schooler menaced by Daleks.

Leaving the foxhound running riot in the kitchen, I went to phone the hunt. I rang six different numbers, but got no reply. Another tip: if you are going to give sanctuary to a misplaced foxhound, try not to do so on the day of the Hunt Ball.

Of the rest of the night, and the baleful howling and the rank stinks that disfigured it, I shall spare you the details. Eventually, at ten the next morning, I raised the Master. Half an hour later, a man in tweed trousers and a tattersall checked shirt rang the doorbell. 'Peevish?' he asked when I opened it. 'Well,' I replied testily, 'I've hardly had a wink of sleep and ...'

The man cocked his head to one side and stared at me as if trying to judge whether I was sane or not. 'Noooo,' he said slowly, 'I think you have one of our hounds. That's her name, Peevish.'

The agricultural community is not generally thought of as lyrical, yet in the naming of foxhounds there is a rich poetry. The names of dogs at hound-trailing events or entered in the canine section at local shows roll down the page like romantic verse: Hamlet, Harkaway, Talisman, Tarquin, Tailer, Dalesman, Gallant, Guardsman, Clarion, Palmer, Grafter, Ranger and Sergeant are the sort of names hunts-men give to their dogs. The bitches' names are softer and, if anything, even more resonant: Honey, Haze, Clover, Cloudy, Beeswing, Moonlight, Bashful and Relish are a few I've come across down the years. Now there was Peevish.

How my guest came by such a moniker I'll likely never know, but I shall probably find myself wondering about it through the years whenever I look at the stains on the porch rug.

I was tired and jaded and wired with coffee when I arrived in Carlisle. The drive from the Tyne Valley to Jedburgh was pretty straightforward, but getting to the town by public transport was complex. You could take two trains to Berwick and then get the bus to Kelso and catch another to Jedburgh, or you could do what I was doing: go to Carlisle, then bus to Galashiels and another one from there to Jedburgh. Either way, it took about five hours and was clearly designed to discourage fraternisation between two sets of people who, from the fourteenth to the seventeenth centuries, had spent a lot of time trying to kill each other.

There was a man standing at the bus stop in Carlisle. He had the shrivelled face of a twice-baked conker and the eyes of a ferret. My train had been delayed and I asked if the X95 had left. The man blew out a cloud of cinnamon-scented vape fumes. 'Nah,' he said in a Border Scots accent that made him sound like he'd been gargling Nitromors. 'He should be here in three minutes, 'less he's stopped in a lay-by for a wank.'

Thankfully the X95 arrived un-delayed by al fresco masturbation and we were soon trundling up through the wild country that had once been so lawless both England and Scotland had abandoned it. For many centuries before Scotland and England were unified – and for several decades afterwards – the Debatable Lands had resounded to the popping of gunfire, the crackle of burning rooftops and the howling of wolves. Things were much quieter now. Except on the bus. One of the surest signs of middle age in a man is the insistence on saying, 'If I were in charge, I'd ...' Quite when this sets in I'm not exactly sure, but I'd say somewhere between nodding in approval at a Jeremy Clarkson column and buying a pair of trousers from an advert in a newspaper colour supplement.

'If I were in charge, I'd ...' is generally followed by an outpouring that combines comedy with fascism. 'If I were in charge, I'd ... ban caravans from travelling during daylight hours ... outlaw eating pasties from a bag in shopping centres ... shoot people who sniff ...'

Being wise to this phenomenon, I have neatly sidestepped it, though the bus journey to Galashiels persuaded me that if I were in charge, I'd jail anyone who watched YouTube clips on public transport without headphones.

At Newcastleton, a short, stocky man in an odd variety of clothes that suggested he'd been shoplifting in Oxfam got on and sat next to me. He gave off what was, to people of my age, the reassuring smell of Silk Cut cigarettes, beer and Old Spice. He asked me where I was going. I told him. I asked him where he was travelling too. 'Hawick,' he said in a voice you could have sanded timber with. 'Scoping out a job. Could be a regular thing.'

I asked him what he did. 'Rodent exterminator,' he said. I imagine that at this point most people stopped questioning him, but I am a pro, after all. 'Is it a busy time of year for you, then?' I asked.

'Oh aye,' the exterminator said. 'Always busy these days.' He said the rat population was getting out of control. This was a boom time for them – and him. Milder winters were one factor and then there was the change in human eating habits. 'People these days chuck out their leftovers,' he said, 'It's not like when we were kids, eh? You never got a meal back then that didn't have a bit of yesterday's dinner in it, did you? You know what they say? In Britain today you are never more than 10 feet from a rat.' He glanced around the bus as if to check how accurate the statistic was.

'So, you're off to the Jedforest sprint, eh?' the Ratman said. He told me he had been many times when he was a child. 'My uncle was a sprinter, you see. Only he had to appear under a false name. He was a winger for Hawick. The rugby union folk took a dim view of players making money from any kind of sport – couldn't even take a few quid for an after-dinner speech. They'd have banned him outright, if they found out what he was up to. So my uncle never ran locally. He went away down to Cumberland or Northumberland. He had to be canny about it. Nobody could know. He told the neighbours he was visiting relatives. His wife was sworn to secrecy. If he won any cash, they tucked it away. If word had got out, well . . .'

That was the truth of professional athletics; it was a clan-destine world. A Northumbrian friend of mine who would eventually get a blue as part of the Cambridge University 4 x 100m relay team used to spend his summer holidays in the late 1950s racing on the pro circuit. 'I had a pseudonym. I gave the address of an old schoolmate who lived in Durham. One summer I even grew a moustache! If the Amateur Athletics Association had found out, I'd have got a life ban.' He said the most he ever earned in prize money was £17 at Haydon Bridge Sports Day one July afternoon. 'But when you were a student that was a lot of money.'

Not that pro sprinting had always been hidden. Writing at the end of the eighteenth century, Joseph Strutt commented that 'in the present day, foot-races are not much encouraged by persons of fortune, and seldom happen but for the purposes of betting and the racers are generally paid for their performance.' During the Georgian and early Victorian eras, pretty much all athletics had been professional. And then came Baron Pierre de Coubertin and the Olympic movement. At first the pros scoffed at the little Frenchman and his silly Corinthian ideals. There was an over-riding feeling amongst them that he was a crank and that while his Olympics might stimulate interest in running in 'southern Europe', it was unlikely to affect anybody in the more sensible nations to the north. Little did they suspect that soon De Coubertin and followers like the ineffable American Avery Brundage (International Olympic Committee president from 1952 to 1972) and Sigfrid Edström (first president of the International Amateur Athletics Federation) would make outlaws of them all.

'Aye, my uncle ran against some of the greats,' the Ratman said. 'Eric Cummings the Australian, first foreigner to win the Powderhall, and Ivor McAnanay, who came out of Blyth. He came up against the Aborigine Wally McArthur, and Brian Bevan, the Aussie rugby league player, who was earning truckloads of money at Warrington at the time. It was quite a world back then. All kinds of shenanigans went on. Running with lead in their shoes. Turning up in disguise. You know what the bookies say? "Never bet on anything that talks."' He let out a great throaty laugh and exited the bus in Hawick, advising me to heed this wise advice.

The Jedburgh Border Games were held at Riverside Park, a stretch of meadowland down by the Jed Water, flanked by a bank of high deciduous trees, that was home to the town rugby club. By the time I'd arrived, the early events – a race around the town and various short sprints for juniors and veterans – had already taken place. There was a scent of trampled grass and fried onions and, as if in response to some biblical injunction demanding their presence at every rural event in Britain, a band of bagpipers.

The Jedburgh Border Games had started in 1853, possibly inspired by the Highland Games, though the Lakeland Games had commenced around the same time, too. They were under the patronage of the 8th Marquis of Lothian, who had the sort of swirling facial hair that called to mind those friends of mine who'd abandoned having a shave during the COVID lockdowns, presumably because their valets didn't live in. The people of the Scottish Borders were noted for being modest and taciturn, so if the Jedburgh Border Games stated that it was 'the Blue Riband Meeting of Scotland's Summer Circuit', you could be sure it was no idle PR boosterism.

The centrepiece of the games was the Jedforest Sprint, which has been run since 1871. When it comes to professional handicap running, the race is arguably the third most important event on the planet after the Powderhall Sprint, which began in 1870 and is run in January at Musselburgh Racecourse near Edinburgh, and Australia's Stawell Gift, which has been staged in the Grampian Mountains of Victoria since 1878.

The Jedburgh race has attracted the greatest professional runners in history. It had been won by, among others, African-American Barney Ewell, the silver medallist in the 100m and

200m at the 1948 Olympics. He captured the prize in 1950 in a time that was a British all-comers record for pros. That summer, Ewell also ran at the Morpeth Olympics and the Keswick Lakeland Sports, as well as at half a dozen meetings in the Borders, all the while lodging in a house in Bathgate. Likeable and charismatic, his appearance at Jedburgh attracted a post-war record crowd of 6,000.

Nowadays, professional handicap running is confined to a narrow circuit of events in the Scottish Lowlands and the Lake District, but there had once been races all over Britain. The Pontypridd 130-yard handicap, called the Great Welsh Sprint, had begun in 1903 and in its heyday had attracted crowds of 40,000 to Taff Vale Park. Many of the Welsh sprinting schools were organised by prize-fighters, among them world flyweight champion Jimmy Wilde, whose pasty skin and punching power led to him being given one of boxing's greatest nicknames: 'The Ghost with the Hammer in his Hand'. Perhaps the greatest betting coup in pro sprinting history was pulled off at Taff Park in 1912 by Peerless Jim Driscoll, a former British and Commonwealth featherweight champion, and his sprinter Mike 'Jake' Crowley. Crowley, who played rugby for Cardiff, had fooled everyone about his potential by running throughout the season wearing a lead-lined belt under his vest. With the odds consequently stacked against him in the final at Pontypridd, Crowley removed the belt and sped to victory earning himself the £100 first prize and Driscoll such a fortune that he paid his runner a bonus of £800.

The coalfields of north-east England were particularly fertile ground for pro running. Northumberland was home of the Morpeth Olympics, an annual showdown between professional athletes that had started back in the 1870s and eventually fizzled out in the 1950s. The Morpeth Olympics 100-yard dash once offered the biggest prize in English sprinting.

The professional athletics circuit was so extensive that runners would come over from Australia and the USA to compete, moving from the Lakeland Sports to the Border meets and to events across Northumberland and Durham. Prizes were huge, big names earned appearance fees and there was a welter of side betting and the possibility of arranging big-money matches. In 1909, Jack Donaldson, the Australian known as 'The Blue Streak', arrived in England and placed adverts in the sporting press offering to take on any runner over any distance from 120 yards to 880 yards for £500 a side. Donaldson's compatriot, Arthur 'The Crimson Flash' Postle, also came to Britain that year. The elegant Postle, whose nickname came from his red silk running gear, is still considered by many experts to be the greatest male Australian sprinter in history.

Alongside big events like those at Jedforest, Pontypridd, Musselburgh and Morpeth, there were hundreds of smaller races in pit villages like Choppington, Seghill, Guide Post and the evocatively named Klondyke. In 1950, for example, 217 men entered the 120-yard handicap sprint at Mickley Flower Show in Northumberland. One of them was my next-door neighbour, John Ferguson. The prize for winning the Mickley Flower Show Sprint was £75. John Ferguson was a police constable. His take-home pay was £3 and 10 shillings a week. One of the men John lined up against was Jackie Milburn, the centre forward for Newcastle United. Jackie Milburn's take-home pay was £14 a week.

At the trackside in Mickley, a row of bookmakers chalked up the odds on the races. Albert Spence from Blyth was the favourite. Spence had won the previous year's Powderhall Sprint, picking up £1,000. He had won the Morpeth Olympics too, as well as finishing second in the Jedforest Sprint. Two years before, he had been working in a ship-yard. Now he trained full-time and ate steak for breakfast. He ran in races all across the north of England and Scotland, at flower and produce shows, Lakeland Sports Days and the Border Games. In the autumn, Spence's backers, a flashy crew of Tyneside publicans, gamblers and bookies, would pay his passage to Australia so he could run in the Victorian Athletic League series that culminated with world's richest foot race, the Stawell Gift. Spence finished third in the Gift, landing himself a pay-out of AU$ 5,000. Nobody knew if his backers were pleased or disappointed. 'Handicap sprinting,' chuckled John Ferguson, 'was the only game in the world where you could get wealthy by losing.'

Spence was not the only one to run full-time. 'If the backers found a prospect,' John Ferguson said, 'some lad from down the pit, they took them off to live in this old RAF station by Silloth in Cumbria. Bleak as buggery, it was.

Nothing to distract them, you see. They'd have a breakfast of poached eggs and what they called a Powderhall chop – a big lamb chop the size of a fella's hand. They went to the gym and hit a punchbag. They got massages. They kipped in the afternoons. They went and practised starting out of the holes – there weren't any blocks back then. In places like Brough Park [a stadium in Byker that's now a greyhound and speedway track], you were running on cinders, so you took a trowel and dug a couple of spots for your feet.'

For miners and other manual workers, the prizes won in handicaps were a big deal. During the 1926 General Strike, one old pitman-sprinter told the author and chronicler of pro running, Frederick Moffatt, that 'the two £10 prizes I won that year kept my family from starvation'. There was big money to be made by backers and bookmakers but, for many competitors, running was about survival. Not all though. The great runners could make what, in those days, amounted to a fortune. 'There was one year in the early 1950s,' my pal the Blue said, 'when Albert Spence won twenty handicap sprints in the Borders alone. He maybe took £400 over a few months just from that small circuit.' A top-flight footballer back then was making around £700 a year. 'When Spence came back from running in Australia in the late 1940s, his backers offered to meet challengers at £1,000 per side. Barely anybody knows about him now, but Spence was a massive deal in that little world, I can tell you.'

During the 1960s, the amount of races fell and the number of competitors dwindled, too. Frederick Moffatt blamed it on a post-war generation, coddled by parents who 'wanted their children to have all the things they had been denied'. Modern youth as a consequence were weak and feckless. This is a familiar refrain. According to recent reports, the government are seriously concerned about the present generation of schoolchildren. Apparently, today's kids are the most overweight and inactive in history. They prefer to come home from a hard day of continual assessment and slump in front of a smartphone or Xbox, rather than engaging in the sort of outdoor pursuits that kept previous generations sharp in body and mind: ringing people's doorbells and running away, lurking round the back of the chip shop firing catapults at stray cats, and riding a bike down the pavement at top speed making machine-gun noises at passers-by and yelling, 'Take that, Fritz!'. That the current school generation is heavy and sluggish is perhaps even more alarming now than it was when Moffatt was writing in the 1970s. Children after all are the future – not least of our state pension. We must ensure they are healthy and vigorous enough to pay income tax, or we'll spend our retirement years eating dog food. Pro sprint-style cash prizes at school sports days might be a start.

Be that as it may, or may not, the fact remained that professional running was a part of British sport you never heard about. It was not polite or genteel; it did not foster a spirit of fair play. Alfred Downer was born in Jamaica to Scottish parents, arguably making him the first of the great Caribbean sprinters. The fastest man in Victorian England, his nickname was The Flying Scotsman. Downer won the

Powderhall Sprint in 1898, covering 128.5 yards in 12.4 seconds. Little wonder the train was named after him. In his book on running, Downer summarised the attitude of the professional. 'When the race starts, there is no man worth his salt that will still be stationary. If there is anything about him, he will already have covered five yards at the call of "Go".'

In Downer's time, competitions were very different from today. A certain amount of decorum prevailed – runners could be disqualified for having dirty legs, for example, and shorts and tops were expected to provide adequate cover of the athlete's limbs and torso, so as not to frighten the horses. In a memorable section of his autobiography *Running Recollections*, Downer focuses on the importance of food in preparing for competition. His advice is unlikely to find favour with those training Dina Asher-Smith or Jake Wightman, but it makes for fascinating reading.

According to Downer, athletes should avoid eating pork, veal and lamb because of their laxative effects, and cheese because it 'curdles the stomach'. Meanwhile, the only liquid it is safe to imbibe is 'strong bitter ale'. In the evening, red wine may be taken, though never – Downer counsels wisely – more than half a pint at a time.

Not content with offering his own advice, Downer also consults the greatest athletes of his era to get their tips on eating. Edgar Chester Bredin ('half-mile champion of the world') suggests that for a pre-race meal 'the inside of a pork chop and a glass of port cannot be beaten'. Meanwhile Len Hurst ('world title holder at 20 miles') countenances as much meat as the athlete can stow away but only a very small amount of vegetables 'since anything inducing flatulence must be avoided'. For the long-distance runner, Hurst declares, fish and water are both to be avoided at all costs 'for both swell the abdomen and injure the breath'.

It is easy to look back at the training methods of athletes of the past with a wry smile and a superior chuckle. And Downer does just that when comparing his own 'scientific' approach to that of the sportsmen of the Georgian era. Captain Robert Barclay – 'world champion pedestrian' of the 1820s, who once walked 1,000 miles in 1,000 hours on Newmarket Heath to settle a bet – prepared for such feats of endurance on a regimen of 'Glaubers' salt' (a 'cathartic agent'), underdone mutton, stale bread, flat ale and frequent steam baths, and purges that, Downer remarks, 'would have reduced any ordinary individual to nothing better than a likely candidate for place of honours in a coffin'.

Barclay, however, was a man of robust constitution. He had inherited it from his paternal line. His grandfather was MP for Kincardine and made a habit of hiking from his constituency in Fife to Westminster for each parliamentary session, enriching himself en route 'with many a prize hat for cudgel play or wrestling'. 'Present members of the house,' Downer notes severely of the politicians of his own era, 'prefer to travel on express trains at 50 miles per hour' (and not a decent cudgel fighter amongst them). Barclay's father did not walk quite as much as his father or his son, but he was a physically imposing man who once impressed workers on his estate by picking up a trespassing horse and hurling it over a hedge. What he ate to build his strength is not recorded, though no doubt he followed Downer's wise advice that 'a good-quality cigar is the best thing to clear the lungs'.

Downer ran as an amateur for most of his career, but only by concealing all the payments he received. In 1887, the Amateur Athletics Association began a campaign to eradicate 'the scourge of professionalism' from running. The government approved. Under new laws, any professional found guilty of posing as an amateur, appearing under a false name, or deliberately losing a race could be sentenced to a year in prison with hard labour.

The measures were prompted by one of the most notorious incidents of the age. In the summer of 1887, the two most famous sprinters of the Victorian era, Harry Gent, a Darlington Hansom cabby, and Harry Hutchens, a London costermonger, were contracted to run against one another in a 120-yard dash at Lillie Bridge Grounds in west London. The purse was £200, winner takes all. Seventeen thousand people paid to watch the race. Behind the scenes, however, tensions surfaced when it became clear that both runners had backed their rival to win. A row ensued. Unable to decide which of them should take a fall, the two runners, their backers and the bookies absconded over a wall with the gate receipts. Incensed, the crowd rioted and burned down the stadium.

Amateurism was thought to purge sport of such unsavoury elements, to wash it clean again. (In 1968, Avery Brundage claimed that 'the principles of fair play and sportsmanship' were 'embodied in the amateur code', even though systematic doping was already widespread.) The Victorians called this new and wholesome version 'rational recreation'. The driving force behind the change was not only the public schools and universities, but also church groups. Methodism in particular had a profound effect in the industrial north where it promoted cricket and football as healthy alternatives to cock-fighting and the like. Cricket and golf managed to tread the line between the old and new worlds by allowing amateurs and professionals to play together. Rugby split into two codes in 1895 (league for professionals, union for amateurs), so did bowls (lawn for amateurs, crown green for pros), the major tennis tournaments would be strictly amateur until the late 1960s, while athletics came to be so dominated by the ideals of De Coubertin, Brundage and their pals that the professional version faded more or less entirely from public view. Under pressure from US TV companies, the International Olympic Committee would finally abandon its stance against professionals in 1986. The International Amateur Athletics Federation started awarding prize money in 1997.

Yet neither the IAAF nor the Olympic movement could ever totally stamp out professional running. It continued and flourished in working-class communities across Britain. When he won the Powderhall Sprint, Albert Spence was probably the fastest man in the world, but – as my friend said – very few people outside the closed circuit of pros have ever heard of him. Athletics records were only for amateurs.

The deeds of the great professionals are missing from the lists as surely as those of drug cheats.

Professional runners were ostracised by what had become the Establishment. Scipio Africanus Mussabini, the London-born pro sprinter, billiard player and sports journalist, would coach Harold Abrahams and five other athletes to Olympic glory, but was never allowed inside the stadium to watch because he was a full-time professional coach (Ian Holm played him in the film *Chariots of Fire*). George McNeil from Tranent in Scotland might have won a gold for Britain in the 1972 Olympics if he hadn't been banned from amateur athletics because, as a seventeen-year-old, he had played three games of professional football for Heart of Midlothian. Barney Ewell, victor at the 1950 Jedforest sprint, had been banned by the Americans shortly after the 1948 Olympics because he'd accepted gifts from fans. (The US athletics authorities used their powers in particularly vindictive ways when it came to non-white athletes. Native American Jim Thorpe was stripped of his 1912 Olympic Gold in the pentathlon after it emerged he had once played semi-pro baseball, while the great Jesse Owens was banned a few months after the Berlin Olympics for receiving endorsements. Celebrated for sticking one to Adolf Hitler and his Aryan supermen, he never raced seriously again.) Downer, too, was banned by the British Amateur Athletics Association. He made considerable money as a professional, but a torn muscle ended his career. His health destroyed by debt, worry and alcohol, The Flying Scotsman died in an asylum aged just thirty-nine.

In the parkland by the Jed Water, the heats of the Jedforest Sprint were nearly done. The competitors were a mixed bunch, young and old, male and female. Professional foot races were run using a handicapping system similar to that in horse racing, except that in professional sprint racing, the handicap is measured in distance rather than in weight. For example, the fastest runners will start a 120-yard sprint at the 120-yard line, slower runners at the 110-yard, 100-yard mark or points in between. As in horse racing, the handicap is based on previous races and times. The handicap system means that – theoretically, at least – every competitor has a chance of winning the race, even if one of the competitors is Usain Bolt. When I'd first watched the Powderhall Sprint back in 1998, a runner named John Bury from Lockerbie reached the final despite being a pensioner. Bury ran the 110-metre race off a handicap of 29 metres – that is to say he ran 81 metres, while the fastest runner in the race, Josephus Thomas of Woodford Green, ran the full 110. Handicapping gave everyone a chance and it allowed women to compete on equal terms with men. The last Jedforest Sprint before COVID had been won by a local teenager, Rianna Sterrick, who'd run off a mark of 21 metres. Sterrick was the third female winner.

Anticipation mounted as the minutes ticked off towards the final. Iskan Barskanmay had won the event way back in 2009, but his handicap seemed to give him a chance to repeat the feat. The Jedforest Sprint was run over 110 metres and Iskan started six metres ahead of the fastest man in the field, Gkontouin Imante. The family behind me were yelling for the tall, dark and handsome local, Cameron Clamp, who was on his marks 4.5 metres ahead of Imante.

I watched for signs. The Blue had told me that sprinting was largely in the head. 'The race is won before the runners even get into their blocks,' he said. 'It's all psychological.' I nodded in agreement when he told me this. The same had been true at my school sports day. Mind you, that wasn't because of any complex mind games. It was just because there was one of those massive, prematurely hairy boys in my year who hated to lose: the 100 metres, the sack race, the egg-and-spoon, it didn't matter. Anyone who beat him would be collared in the changing rooms afterwards and have his head stuck in the toilet. I don't suppose this was ever a worry for people like Lamont Marcell Jacobs, or any of the competitors today. Back in the past, it seemed like something the bookies might have gone for, but things were less feisty now.

The runners came to their positions. The starter called his instructions. Silence fell. The gun bang echoed through the trees, sending crows scattering. Clamp overhauled Iskan at the halfway point and held off a late surge by Imante to breast the tape first. He stood for a moment panting, then raised his arms and cracked into the beaming smile of a man who had just earned himself £3,000 in less than 12 seconds.

10

Cake, Rattle and Bowl

SKITTLES, SOMERSET

The farrier came from over by Accrington. He had an accent so soft and mild it would have soothed a teething baby. He said, 'I did my training down in Somerset. We finished on a Friday night after a week's graft. I said, "Where are we off tonight, lads?" And these Somerset lads, they just shook their heads. They said, "Oh, no. It's skittles night tonight. We're playing. We never go out on a skittles night. Never."'

He rolled his eyes. 'Seemed to be the same every night. Tuesday, Wednesday. "We've got skittles." They were bloody mad for skittles, those Somerset boys.' He paused for a moment, his eyes staring off into the distant past, his brow furrowed. 'Either that,' he said eventually, 'or they didn't much care for my company.'

I had never heard of men playing skittles when I was young. This was because skittles' main rival for popularity has always been quoits. The two games never flourished side by side. It is either one or the other. There never seems to have been much interest in skittles in North Yorkshire, Durham and Northumberland, while quoits has been unerringly popular. Likewise in Somerset, where skittles rules, nobody seems to know a clay end from a hole in the ground.

The only time I'd ever been in a skittles alley was somewhere in Devon during a holiday in the 1980s. I was with a friend who'd been a junior javelin thrower of some local repute. When he saw the skittles, he got very excited. He hurled the cheese with the vigour of an Olympic athlete. The noise was horrendous. It was as if some mad giant was batting away at a massive, out-of-tune glockenspiel with huge woodworking mallets. 'They should have given us some ear defenders,' I said to my friend. He shook his head. 'No, it was last Friday, I think.' Skittles, it is fair to say, is not a game you could play secretly.

This had been a bit of an issue for long periods of its history because skittles is probably the most banned game in British history. Attempts to suppress it have been long, brutal and bloody. But no matter what actions were taken against it, no matter what obstacles – legal, economic or social – were put in its way, skittles just could not be stopped. Mankind will find a cure for the common cold long before anyone finally does away with skittles. It is the cockroach of games, only in a good way.

The invention of skittles is usually attributed to those Christian monks who were given the unenviable task of bringing the wild tribes of Germany to Christ during the Dark Ages. The skittles were, so legend has it, originally made from the wooden clubs the German barbarians carried for self-defence. Called a kegel, the club had a flattened top, which it could be stood on. The monks seemed to have used skittles to illustrate Christian principles, possibly in the same way that the Second World War soldier boy did in the Tex Ritter hit song 'The Deck of Cards' (the G. I. in question was apparently unable to play a hand of cribbage without delivering a sermon about wick-trimming virgins, washed lepers and the like, doubtless to the delight of any betting man in the vicinity), though quite how that would have worked is hard to fathom.

For a long while in England, the words 'bowls' (aiming at a jack) and 'skittles' were interchangeable. As bowls developed the need for a flat lawn on which to play, it tended to limit its appeal. Skittles, which could be played on pretty much any surface, became hugely popular.

There were almost as many variations in skittles as there are words to express drunkenness in the English language. The style of skittles the farrier's workmates had been playing was Western skittles. Western skittles is the most popular form of the game in the UK, though as the name suggests its players mainly live in Somerset, Devon, Gloucestershire, Dorset, Herefordshire and anywhere else you can imagine The Wurzels having a pint of scrumpy. Oh, and South Wales, too. Western skittles emerged as a distinct game in the late Middle Ages. We know this not because of archaeological evidence, but from the early attempts to put a stop to what the authorities seemed to agree was a menace to society. The first such attempt was made by royal edicts in 1511. In 1541, Henry VIII severely reinforced the prohibition while at the same time playing the game very keenly himself and having alleys built in his palace at Whitehall. The Big Man did exactly the same thing when it came to bowls. The prohibition on both games applied only to those who didn't have a landed income of over £100 a year. Some might view this as hypocritical, but I have a feeling Henry felt that if there wasn't one law for the rich and another for the poor, then the legal system wasn't working properly.

As a consequence of the ginger bigamist's intervention from the mid-sixteenth century, having a skittle alley at your home became something of a status symbol, matched only by that of having your own dovecote. Owning a skittles alley was visible proof of your earnings – like driving a Tesla.

The poorer Englishman had to confine himself to archery practice, or play the prohibited game and risk getting caught and fined 6 shillings and 8 d (about 33p). The number of fines handed out across England suggests that many, many people were prepared to take that risk. In a bid to halt the devilment, the fines increased in number and severity as the sixteenth century moved towards its conclusion. In *The School of Abuse* from 1579, Stephen Gossen warned that skittle alleys were 'privy mothers that eat up the credit of many idle citizens, whose gaines at home are not able to weigh down their losses abroad'. Skittles, Gossen fulminated, took bread from the mouths of wives and children, and ruined businesses. In Scotland, the authorities took an equally dim view of the game. In 1660, a fine of 10 shillings could be imposed on anyone playing on the Sabbath.

By the time of the Restoration, the longbow had been replaced with the matchlock musket, archery practice was no longer essential for the safety of the nation and the Puritans had been banished. In the merry England of Charles II, skittles was seen as a healthy country pursuit and, along with its cousin bowls, became the most popular sport in the land (cricket had yet to make a full appearance and football was still the pagan stuff of Shrove Tuesday melees).

Yet despite its mass appeal, or possibly because of it, the War on Skittles continued much as the War on Drugs does today. Attempts to put a stop to the game were as forceful as the efforts to eradicate cocaine and evidently just as futile. In 1752, for example, Francis Hales, the mayor of Manchester, issued an order to suppress all skittle grounds, ninepin alleys and tennis courts in the city. In 1762, constables in Suffolk ransacked local public houses looking for illegal alleys. In 1784, the mayor and justices of Hereford ordered that 'all persons keeping any skittle alley, tennis or fives-court are forthwith required to take up or destroy them'. And on it went.

According to Joseph Strutt, a common belief among skittles players was that the law specifically forbade only the game that was named, so that by simply calling it something else they could carry on with impunity. Unfortunately for them, magistrates took the view that skittles was skittles even if you called it Thatcher's Malarkey or Nine-Toed Frottage and fined them accordingly. By the time Strutt arrived in London in the 1770s, skittle alleys had been, he says, 'totally abolished' in the capital.

I travelled south to see what all the fuss had been about, to watch a match in Taunton, a place that was to skittles what Milton Keynes is to roundabouts. The St Austell Brewers Skittle League had recently reached its exciting climax, but luckily for skittles addicts, the winter league was no sooner finished than the summer league had begun. I had come to the Princess Royal, a solid, square Edwardian pub a few hundred yards from the county cricket ground that had not one but two alleys, to watch a game between the home side, Jonno's Boys, and the visitors, Piston Broke. The skittles teams mainly had jokey names – The Pink Pythons, Pin Pricks and the like – though the players hadn't put quite so much effort and imagination into thinking of puns as they do in local five-a-side football leagues, where you're likely to find Surreal Madrid taking on Club Tropicana Drinks FC.

Mercifully, temperatures in England had returned to relative normality. A week or so earlier, I'd been with friends to see England play South Africa at Chester-le-Street. The last one-day international we'd watched together at the Riverside had been memorable for the fact that it had been so cold that, just before the start of play, a man sitting near us pulled out a sleeping bag and got into it. We spent the rest of the day shivering and looking at him with envy. This time the sun beat down so fiercely that England fast bowler Matthew Potts went off after six overs with possible heat stroke. Behind us, a bloke came back from the bar with two glasses of Pimms. 'I asked for water,' his mate said. The first bloke sighed. 'Aye, I know, but they've run out of water and this was the nearest.' Later, people were being wheeled off on stretchers with drips in their arms. It was so grimly, oppressively sweaty that not a single red-faced, middle-aged man said, 'If this is climate change, I'm all for it,' which, like the temperatures themselves, was likely a UK record.

The Princess Royal was bustling for a midweek evening. By the service hatch, a waitress was laughing about dropping a frozen pea down the chef's back. Two women in joggers and leopard-print were sitting at a corner table. One said, 'He loved beer that much that when he bought a collie, he called it Firkin. He hadn't thought that through, had he? Now when it runs off you can hear him all over the village bellowing, "Firkin come here! Firkin get in!" It's a wonder nobody's called the police.'

Western skittles is played between teams of eight over seven hands (rounds of three throws per player). There are nine pins, all about 10 inches tall except for the king pin which, naturally enough, is taller. An individual match score of 80 is the equivalent of scoring a hat-trick in football, while a team total of over 520 will likely earn a headline in the local newspaper.

The pitch is 2 yards wide and between 9 and 13 yards in length. It is floored with oak boards or, in a touch that World of Interiors would surely approve, strips of maple veneer.

Generally, the alley surface is flat, but in some cases it is cambered after the style favoured in the skittle alleys of Flanders and Holland. The game is very popular in the Low Countries. In Belgium, they even play an ancient variation that was once a favourite of East Anglians: half-bowl or rolly-polly. Half-bowl – which doesn't require an alley – got its name because the ball or bowl that was thrown at the skittles had literally been cut in half. This meant that it followed a curved path when rolled in much the same way – if more haphazardly – than weighted bowls woods do today.

Instead of being aimed at nine or ten pins, the half-bowl was aimed at fifteen or sixteen. The game was popular in Essex and Suffolk, but died out in the early twentieth century. It clung on in the French-speaking southern half of Belgium. Here it is called Rolle Bolle and, judging by the YouTube clips I have watched, is played by men who pretty much answer the same description.

The balls are made of lignum vitae (a hardwood from the West Indies that is so heavy a cargo of 100 logs is pretty much enough to sink most ships), hornbeam or alder and weigh about 5 pounds. In some places, solid rubber balls are used, which makes the game much quieter. As an outsider, I'd say that maybe foam skittles and a cork floor might work, too. Sitting and watching, the game was as ferociously noisy as it had been the only time I'd played it. The echoing sound of wood striking wood seemed even more of a guarantee of a ringing skull than the cider I was drinking.

At least I was seeing a game, though. I'd not had the same

luck when it came to watching Britain's second favourite form of skittles: long alley. This is a rugged version of the game played with a 4lb lump of wood that is called a cheese, though it looks more like a bomb, in an alley that is 35 feet long and 6 feet wide. It's surfaced with cobbles for the first eight paces beyond the bowler's mark and then with heavy plank boards, railway sleepers, slate or tarmac. In Western skittles, the ball is bowled along a smooth surface. In long alley skittles, the surface is rough and the cheese is thrown and bounces at odd angles. As a result, long alley is more violent and primal. It looks like a Viking-version of skittles and, in Victorian times, the faint of heart and the sickly were warned to avoid it for fear they would suffer an attack of the vapours.

Unsurprisingly, this rough-hewn game was popular in the same neck of the woods that produced Sporty Payne and the bottle-kickers – Leicestershire, Nottinghamshire, Derbyshire and Northamptonshire. I'd aimed to take the opportunity of visiting Hallaton to catch a game of long alley skittles at the Railway Arms at nearby Kibworth Beauchamp, a name that suggested to me a murder suspect in a Hercules Poirot mystery. Sadly, I based my choice of venue on old information and arrived only to find that the Railway Arms had been dolled up in 2019, the bowling alley ripped out and replaced with a restaurant. The gammon, egg and chips was decent enough, but plainly no substitute for watching a group of ex-pitmen hurling a mighty cheese at nine oak skittles in the hope of making 'a whack up' (knocking down all nine pins with one throw) and avoiding 'a monkey face' (missing the skittles with all three throws). At least this non-event served to illustrate the frailty of this rugged old game. Long alley venues were being disposed of at such an alarming rate that many wondered about the future. If things continue as they are, some experts believe a game that has been played since the days of the Saxons will have disappeared for good by the mid-point of the current century. Still, campaigners have successfully brought back the beaver and the great bustard, so I guess there is hope.

The game in Taunton literally rattled along. The players came and went. At one point, the entire visiting squad exited for the bar, trusting their opponents to keep score accurately without being overseen. Pistons took an early lead, having thrown with greater consistency. In Somerset, the ball was chucked one-handed and underarm, often at the sort of ferocious speed a West Indian paceman might envy. This was not true in neighbouring Dorset where the ball was generally thrown two-handed like a rugby ball. The manoeuvre was complex and athletic – a weird froggy-leap forward with the player releasing when he or she was at full stretch and parallel to the ground. It concluded with a kind of handspring. Known as the Dorset Flop, it looked like one of those moves that might have cropped up in an early 1980s breakdancing film.

The pins – once traditionally made of wood from cider apple trees – had to be constantly put back in place. This job was tackled by a youngster in a red polo shirt, who had the alertness of a whippet and moved with a machine-like precision. The task is a paid position, though it doesn't pay much, which is how we come by the expression 'pin money'. If they don't have a pro to perform the task, a player will have to 'stick up for himself'.

With the game reaching its midpoint, I headed off to the bar to clear my head, which felt as if someone had placed a fire-bucket over it and struck it a dozen times with a lump hammer. The Princess Royal was a large sprawling pub that also had darts and pools teams. In many ways, darts was the sport that skittles might have been. Western skittles had dozens of variations from place to place and league to league. In Poole in Dorset, for instance, three balls of differing weights are thrown in ascending order. In Bath, the ball doesn't have to bounce before hitting the skittles. In some parts of the West Country, the kingpin is placed in the centre of the diamond; in others at the front. Occasionally the kingpin is worth more points than the other skittles. Some leagues discount rebounds off the sides of the alley, others allow them. The size of the pins and the material used to make them varies. In South Wales, the 'Glamorgan pins' are slim, bottle-shaped, around 10 inches tall and made of solid plastic. In Somerset, pins tend to be barrel-shaped and stocky, like a front-row forward. In Bristol, they are the same shape but thinner round the middle, like a front row forward trying to impress a lady.

Up until the 1920s, darts had been much the same. Then, in 1924, all that was changed by a man named Ted Leggatt. Leggatt was an industrial chemist who invented and patented a dartboard made out of plasticine, which proved, possibly quite literally, to be a flop. That same year, he set up the National Darts Association in a pub in Holborn in London.

When Leggatt started his organisation, darts was a game with as many bewildering regional variations as skittles. Most parts of England had their own style of board, for instance. In Staffordshire, what we'd now think of as the outer ring on the bullseye – worth twenty-five points – was represented by two diamonds set between the numbers 14 and 9, and 4 and 13. In Kent, the outer doubles ring counted as trebles with another ring inside for doubles. In Yorkshire, perhaps predictably, the board had no trebles on it and no twenty-five-point bullseye ring.

The NDA started out small but very quickly established themselves as the game's arbiters in much the way the Football Association had done. They standardised the board – the one we know today is the original London version – and the game rules: three darts per throw, best of three games the winner, and set the score at 301, a total that could easily be counted by the scorer on that standard accoutrement of every English pub, a cribbage board.

When the NDA organised its first major tournament at the Red Lion in Wandsworth in London in 1926, it proved such a massive hit that Britain's best-selling newspaper, the *News of the World*, immediately signed up to sponsor the next one. Soon the regional variations of darts had been all but obliterated. Some people, including T. H. White – author of *The Sword in the Stone* – were incensed by what they regarded as the hijacking of an ancient and beloved game by a bunch of bumptious Cockney bureaucrats. White detested what he saw as this further homogenisation of British life. He thought we needed the sporting equivalent of bio-diversity. Maybe he had a point. But try telling that to the crowds today at Ebbsfleet, Frimley Green or the Alexandra Palace.

The closest skittles ever came to having anything like the NDA was back around the same time and in the same city. Skittles had made a comeback in London since Joseph Strutt's time. In the 1930s, there were more than 200 alleys in the capital's pubs. Whereas other skittles were as unruly and ungoverned as an Alaskan river, London skittles had a powerful governing body – the Amateur Skittles Association. Probably to howls of outrage from T. H. White and other drinkers at the Eagle and Child Pub in Oxford, the ASA standardised the rules of the sport, organised tournaments and ensured media exposure. They even crowned a world champion. In 1933, this was Charles Hillier of Tufnell Park, whose victory was considered worthy of coverage by Pathé News.

London skittles was characterised by the use of a 'ball' that was the size and shape of a Christmas cake, made from lignum vitae, and weighed in at around 10 pounds. The pins were barrel shaped. The alley short at around 21 feet. The writer A. P. Herbert was a big fan of skittles and often extolled the virtues of the game in his column in *Punch* magazine, where he likened the sport to something from Ancient Greece (the cheese is a bit like a discus, I guess) and claimed the big matches had an epic quality worthy of *The Iliad*.

The game was played across London, particularly in areas close to the Thames – Barnes, Brentford, Mortlake, Putney and Hammersmith – and out in Surrey towns such as Guildford. The most famous skittles alley was the one at Herbert's local, the Black Lion in Hammersmith. The alley here attracted a glamorous celebrity following with actors Michael Redgrave and Douglas Fairbanks Jr popping in for matches. One of the star players, Cyril Pennington-Richards, was a film cameraman who worked on movies such as *The Wooden Horse* and *The Invisible Man*.

For a brief while it looked like the ASA might lead a revolution, but as Samuel Weller remarked, 'life is not all porter and skittles'. The bubble of excitement surrounding the game was burst abruptly by the Second World War. A number of the most famous skittle pubs in London were destroyed in the Blitz and when peace returned, publicans seeking ways to increase revenue ripped out the alleys and replaced them with restaurants or function rooms (which is what happened at the Black Lion). These days there are only two London skittle alleys left; one at the Freemason's Arms in Hampstead and the other in Norbury. Asked about the situation by the *Independent* in 1996, one of the Hampstead skittlers commented poignantly that 'we are like a pair of mating dodos'.

Without a national governing body, skittles continued as it always had. The variations are both the strength and weakness of the game. It thrives because it is parochial, the players allowed to go about their business unfussed by the sort of centralised blazered bureaucracy that makes life hell for most other sportspeople. On the other hand, the lack of any uniform set of rules means organising any equivalent of a national competition, or even promoting the sport nationally, is impossible. Skittles remains defiantly a local game for local people. And there are a lot of them. The game is played by both men and women, and advancing years are no barrier to competing. An old Movietone documentary film from the 1930s shows four old men with a combined age of 357 playing a game at Bradford Abbas in Dorset (thankfully none of these bearded old codgers attempts the Dorset Flop). There are estimated to be 150 leagues in south-west England and South Wales. Some have only half a dozen sides, the biggest more than 100. Some estimates put the number of players involved at the start of the new millennium as high as 50,000. In 2019, Sport England calculated it as being nearer to 6,500. As Ken Carling from the once-vast Cardiff & District League, which had shrunk so badly in the last decade there was talk of merging with other local leagues, remarked mournfully, 'it is something of a dying art, unfortunately. It's getting too old at the top with not enough young players coming through.'

There was little sign of such melancholy in the alley at the Princess Royal. The players were hurling the ball even more robustly than before and the language was on the Bessemer converter side of industrial. Waves of banter more or less unintelligible to the interloper crashed against the walls and rebounded as gurgles of laughter. Piston Broke had been leading for most of the match, but with the home side's Jez Eagle hitting a purple patch, Jonno's Boys started to claw their way back into it. There were shouts and claps and salty insults between the clatter.

These days, games were played purely for pride and the possibility of placing a shield or cup on the shelf of your local, but back in the Victorian era much money was to be made by those who excelled at skittles. In 1864, the *Norfolk Chronicle* reported on a match at the Wheatsheaf Hotel in King's Lynn between Ben Sexton of Norwich and Fred Strong of Islington for £25 a side and a silver cup. When George Piercey of Isleworth in Middlesex died in 1890, his obituary noted that he had been one of the greatest skittles player, of his age and as a young man in the 1840s had travelled to Newcastle upon Tyne and played a three-game match that 'netted him the sum of £600'.

Top skittles players made a living through gambling (there's evidence that some players moved from town to town as skittle-sharpers, hustling bets at local alleys), or by under-taking 'challenges', such as when Jem Garwood, described as the 'Champion Skittle Player of the World', vowed to 'knock down 1,200 pins and run a mile inside one hour' at the Rose and Crown Inn in Ilford in 1891. Remarkably, he made it with a couple of minutes to spare, securing himself a deal of money from those who had paid to watch and those who had bet against him.

Other skittle champions joined the showmen in wandering around the pleasure fairs and wakes of Britain. In the 1870s, Sexton found himself sharing space with 'The Young Giant Horse', 'The Red Hot Fiery Man' and 'The Spotted African

Lady'. Sexton apparently trumped these attractions by knocking down eighty pins with ten throws with a man standing on his head in the centre of the frame to obstruct him.

In the alley of the Princess Royal, Jonno's Boys took the last hand with a score of seventy; they'd won the previous one with the same total too. Alas, it was not quite enough. When the totals were tallied, Piston Broke had triumphed by four points.

I walked back to my box hotel. From the bedroom window, I could see the twinkling lights of what seemed like an insult to West Country life – the equivalent of raising the Union flag above the Bastille on 14 July, or putting chives in your cheese scones and then entering them for a WI baking competition. For there, winking at me from across the A358, was a sign for the Hollywood Bowl, a ten-pin bowling alley.

Ten-pin bowling is a US version of skittles. Legend has it the tenth pin was added in Connecticut in the 1840s to circumvent a state ban on nine-pin alleys. The first commercial ten-pin alley didn't appear in the UK until 1960, but long before that Edward, Prince of Wales (the infamous Beastly Bertie who become King Edward VII) had had an American-style bowling alley installed at Sandringham, apparently having been taken with one he had seen at the Duke of Sutherland's gaff at Trentham. From this it seems clear that what fashionable gentlemen needed to pass their leisure hours had little changed since the days of the Tudors, albeit that shotguns had replaced longbows as the weapons of choice for killing birds.

The future of skittles worried the older players in Wales and concerned those in the East Midlands, but there were small signs of revival. The number of players logged by Sport England had increased year on year since 2012, and skittle alleys were no longer being ripped out of pubs in the West Country at the rate they had been twenty years ago.

In the eighteenth century, the writer A. Jones had taken a stand against the prevailing view that skittles was a menace to society. Proving that Britain has forever been heading to Hades in a wheelbarrow, he wrote in his book *The Art of Playing at Skittles* of the foppish new generation in 'an over-fed age of people insipid with ease and sloth'. Playing skittles, Jones believed, would save the English from becoming a race with 'bog-bellies, swelled legs, gouty feet and the other ailments of the loaded corpse'. Who knows, it still might.

11

Big Rocks and Shortbread

THE HEAVY SPORTS, SCOTTISH HIGHLANDS

I had been hoping to stay somewhere in what I feel duty-bound to call the Royal Valley of the Dee. I'd had a holiday there in between the first and second lockdowns and had taken inspiration from the sight of the house in Braemar where Robert Louis Stevenson had lived while writing *Treasure Island*. I had pictured the author staring out of the window as the wind howled and snow swirled, imagining himself in the Caribbean. Perhaps predictably, the prices of accommodation in the Royal Valley of the Dee during a global pandemic and the prices when things had – excepting for war in Ukraine and the collapse of the economy – returned to normality were as wide as a spiv's tie, so I had to settle for a box hotel in Aberdeen instead. Still, it had tea and coffee-making facilities and a Corby trouser press, which was a comfort. I have, I should say, never used a trouser press, but as I've got older

I've found the presence of one in a strange town as reassuring as a nightlight is to a fretful child.

I caught the bus out to the west bright and early. The two people on board who were wearing masks looked like members of some sect of old believers. When a man behind me coughed, not a single person looked around with terror and accusation in their eyes. My doctor friend's prophecy seemed to have come true – the fear had faded, a nightmare drifting away to nothingness in the daylight.

The bus was a double decker and thundered along the road oblivious to the overhanging trees, the branches of which thumped and hammered on the roof like the failing limbs of some mad ogre. By the time I alighted in Aboyne, I felt like I'd spent a night in a skittles alley.

Aboyne is a lovely place. Beside it the silvery Dee twinkled as if auditioning for a part in a William McGonagall poem. Like all the villages in the Royal Valley of the Dee, it seemed determined to imprint its civilisation amid the wildness of the surrounding mountains. The gardens were primped and trimmed, the houses spick and span. Everything was neat and in good order. Aboyne looked like the lid of a Christmas shortbread assortment box. It even had a nice pub, which was something of a rarity around these parts. The Scots, possibly due to Presbyterianism, generally seemed to take a dim view of licensed premises and appeared determined to make them as cheerless as possible. A few years earlier, looking for a drink in a nearby town, I'd ended up in a one-storey inn with an interior – fluorescent strip lights, venetian blinds, walls painted a shade of queasy green – that put me in mind of a 1970s betting shop, albeit without the bonus of being able to steal a stubby biro. It was a place that seemed designed to make anyone drinking in it feel both wicked and depressed simultaneously. The man sitting next to me was drinking milk which, judging by the expression on his face, had turned several days earlier. The landlord exuded all the warmth of an iceberg and had the forbidding look of a Cromwellian witch-finder. I had a feeling that if I asked what flavour of crisps were on offer he'd have replied, 'locusts and blood'. I didn't stop long.

The Aboyne Highland Games took place on the sizeable village green, which was big enough to support several rugby pitches. It had run since 1867 and, until the pandemic, only the two world wars had caused its suspension. Now it was back and there was a surging feeling of cheeriness and hope in the air alongside the sound of bagpipes, the screeching of kids on the fairground rides and the smell of crushed turf and malt whisky.

Aboyne prided itself on being the most traditional of Highland Games. Run under the patronage of the Most Honourable the Marquis of Huntly, it had a list of patrons that read like the cast from *Brigadoon*. My particular favourite was the pleasingly minimalist Lilburn of Coull, who I imagine fending off all attempts to give him or her a forename with the words, 'No need for a load of bloody fuss and nonsense. I'm not a damned Frenchman.'

The heavy events had already begun with the light stone

for eighteen- to twenty-eight-year-olds (maturity comes late in the Highland Games), the weight by rings and the 16-pound light hammer. I was particularly taken with the hammer throwing. Or, more specifically, with what they are throwing.

According to the history books, the hammer throw traces its origins to the fifteenth-century hobby of chucking sledgehammers. I think this is unlikely. I should imagine the hammer throw actually came about through many decades of handymen and DIY enthusiasts lobbing the hammer aside with a frustrated yelp of 'How am I supposed to bang a nail in with this bloody thing?'. Because, let's face it, the hammer that is hurled about by the burly Olympic denizens of 'the cage' is not a hammer at all, but an obscene parody. It is a 16-pound iron ball attached to what appears to be a surplus emergency handle from an old railway carriage by 4 feet of spring steel. It has more in common with soap-on-a-rope than it does with the popular woodworking tool. If you went down to your local B&Q and asked to see their entire hammer selection – claw, lump, ball and all – I doubt you would be presented with anything that bore even the remotest resemblance to what passes for a hammer in athletics circles. Yet despite the fact that the case against this bogus object is as plain as the nose on Pinocchio's face, the International Olympic Committee allows the shabby spectacle of the 'hammer' to continue unchecked. No wonder ordinary people are becoming sickened by the whole unsavoury business.

Just as in the 1980s, when the cynical commercialisation

of rock'n'roll led many people to turn their attention back to more traditional musical forms, so nowadays many sports fans are taking an increased interest in the sporting equivalent of world music: 'roots' events such as the Highland Games.

The Highland Games is the Olympics unplugged. It is acoustic athletics. What is more, the tartan-clad giants of the Highland Games still have enough self-respect left to throw a hammer that actually looks like a hammer: a big lump of metal stuck on the end of a stick.

Like many of the Highland Games' heavy events, the hammer throw has martial origins. The first reference to a Highland Games is back in the eleventh century when King Malcolm organised a running race, possibly as a means of selecting men to act as royal couriers. The Ceres Games in Fife dates back to 1314 when Robert the Bruce granted the villagers the right to hold a fair and market as a reward for the part they played in the victory at Bannockburn.

The hammer is a round metal ball weighing around 20 pounds that's attached to a 4-foot stick. Apparently the idea of throwing it dates back to the days when King Edward I of England banned the Scots from carrying weapons. The hammer didn't count, except of course if you bashed somebody over the head with it. But if Edward had taken that attitude, he'd have outlawed chisels, mallets and cake knives.

The tossing of the caber – a 15- to 22-foot trunk from a larch or Scots pine – was believed to stem from siege warfare, where the caber would be tossed up against a castle wall so that warriors could scale up it and over the battlements.

You could likely make a similar case for the event that sees a 56-pound weight lobbed over a high bar one-handed, too. And for the sheaf-toss that sees 20 pounds of straw bundled up in a burlap sack and tossed high over the bar with a pitch-fork, I imagine that in the sort of medieval sword-and-shield epics I watched on Saturday nights as a kid, they would have set light to it first and inside the castle Hollywood extras would have caught it alight and run around screaming until they fell into a well.

While waiting for the heavy events, I went for a wander around the rest of the site. More than 10,000 people had come to Aboyne for the games. The sky was grey and occa-sionally made a half-hearted attempt to rain. It had been hot and sunny for weeks and the grass on the village green had a yellowish tinge. Hills coated in evergreens rose up on the far side of the valley. The banners of various clan chieftains fluttered in the breeze and a pipe band played a stirring march that put me in mind of a Celtic version of the theme from *Thunderbirds*.

Between 1746 and 1782, the British government suppressed the culture of the Highlands even down to the wearing of traditional dress. The Braemar games were first staged in 1832, but may date back 1,000 years. Queen Victoria was a big fan and the games were arranged to fit in with her visits to Balmoral, which generally coincided with the grouse-shooting season that begins on 12 August. The future Widow of Windsor made her first visit to Braemar in 1836. Evidently having enjoyed the sight of lots of muscular young men in vests and kilts striving and straining, she returned every year. Her commitment to the games made them fashionable and, more importantly, respectable. They have gone from strength to strength ever since, spreading all over the world to wherever there was a Scottish population, or even a population who wished they were Scottish. The best-attended games are in the USA and Canada, but there are events in even the most unlikely and least Highland places you can imagine. The only other Highland Games I've ever seen were in Belgium where a fair percentage of the population use the Celtic history of Ambiorix, King of the Belgae ('Of all the Gauls the Belgae are the bravest,' Julius Caesar noted) as a means of proving they are, spiritually at least, Irish or Scottish. 'That's just like how I feel in my heart, you know,' middle-aged Flemish men will tell you after a few beers. If you are really unfortunate, they will then launch into a tearful rendition of 'The Bonnie Banks o' Loch Lomond'.

Like the agricultural shows, the Highland Games had expanded over the years. Aboyne had added the funfair just after the First World War, though they imposed a ban on the playing of 'mechanical music' while the bagpiping, fiddle-playing and dancing events were going on. There were dozens of craft stalls – two words that strike terror into even the bravest among us – alongside some tasty-looking food stands with queues that were as long and winding as a beer-glass snake at an Ashes Test. I paused to look at the caber that would be used in what was the day's star event, the Aboyne caber challenge. The caber had been 'dedicated' to the games a few years earlier by Queen Elizabeth II, who had a little country place just up the road at Balmoral. (Indeed, when I was in Braemar, I'd been having lunch at the swishy Fife Arms when Camilla Parker-Bowles turned up with her security detail and – this revelation may shock you – totally ignored the anti-Covid one-way system.) The first prize for the winner of the caber event was £700.

The Highland Games had never aspired to the Corinthian ideals of amateurism that had infected traditional track and field, though the running events conformed to the rules of the Amateur Athletics Association and prizes were discreetly handled. The sprinting in particular had once been of a very high standard. Trinidad-born Emmanuel McDonald Bailey – an Olympic 100-metre medallist for Great Britain – had set a Scottish all-comers' 100-yard record at the Inverness Gathering of 1950, a mark that was passed the following year at the Edinburgh Highland Games at Murrayfield by the American Andy Stanfield, who went on to win a brace of golds at the Helsinki Olympics a year later.

At Aboyne, there was still a total prize fund of £16,000 on offer for everything from the big throwing events to foot races that ranged from 100 yards to the big 6-mile fell race. In 2019, most of the prizes in the heavy section had been hoovered up by Austria's Lukas Prettenthaler, Polish strongman Lukasz Wenta and Scott Rider, a shot-putter from Kent who'd once been a member of the British Olympic bobsled team. These foreign interlopers were part of a long tradition.

At Braemar, the stone-throwing filled the position the

caber-toss did at Aboyne. Competitors were not allowed to run up or to spin and they had to wear a kilt of their clan tartan. The stone weighs 28 pounds. It was picked from a nearby river bed, presumably by somebody with a wheelbarrow. The record for throwing the stone was once set by English shot-putter and world's strongest man contestant, Geoff Capes (who, I feel obliged to blurt out by forces beyond my control, was also a keen breeder of budgerigars). Back in the 1980s, you could hardly switch on the TV without seeing the Cambridgeshire police officer pulling a truck, lifting a pile of bricks or chucking a vast object an improbable distance. As well as being a double European and Commonwealth shot-put champion, Capes also won the World's Strongest Man and World Muscle Power championships. In the Highland Games' heavy events, he was pretty much invincible during the 1980s. He won his first world title in 1981 in the distinctly un-Scottish venue of Lagos in Nigeria. Bearded and ferocious-looking, Capes – who I also feel compelled to report has the middle name of Humberg – stands 6 ft 6 tall, and weighs about the same as a Fiat 500.

The Cambridgeshire copper was following in the considerable boot-prints of another Great Britain shot-putter who had carved out a considerable reputation in Scotland twenty years earlier. Arthur Rowe was born in Barnsley and worked as a blacksmith at a coalmine, training for athletics behind his local pub using weights made from the wheels of pit wagons. He was British champion five times over and also won golds at the Commonwealth and European championships in the 1950s. Things went sour for Rowe at the 1960 Rome Olympics where the burly Yorkshireman was tipped to become the first British athlete to win a throwing medal since 1924. Alas, the burning heat and the foreign food proved too much for him; he lost close to 10 pounds in weight in a week and failed to qualify for the final. Disillusioned and broke, Rowe quit the rarefied world of amateur athletics shortly afterwards and went to play rugby league for Oldham, earning himself such a signing-on bonus he could buy a house with it. He was big and strong and athletic, but he turned out not to be much good at rugby and his career lasted barely a year.

The Highland Games attracted the best competitors by handing them brown envelopes stuffed with cash. That was information which caught Rowe's attention. 'Maybe if you have gone to Eton or Oxford,' he said, 'you can afford to turn down such offers. If like me you haven't any brass, you take backhanders.' He made his debut at the Braemar Games wearing a borrowed kilt and promptly broke the record for putting the stone by 9 feet. After that, the offers and the money flowed in. At his peak in the mid-'60s, Rowe was being paid £30 per event, a substantial sum in the days when an experienced office worker might take home £15 a week. Any prizes Rowe won – trophies, clocks, ornaments – went immediately to the pawnshop. His response to any offer of an engagement was apparently always 'How much?' and he would ignore the big crowds of the historic Highland Games and perform at a village fete if the money was better.

Rowe struck up a fierce yet paradoxically amiable rivalry with Big Bill Anderson, a great slab of a man from Bucksburn in Aberdeenshire, who trained on a diet of mince and tatties and worked out in his garage during the winter months. The two pushed each other to greater and greater performances. They also became firm friends. In one famous incident after a rainy day of competition at Lochearnhead, the two giants lifted a local newspaperman's car that had sunk in the mud 'as easily as if they were popping a cork from a bottle'.

Like Rowe, the Highland Games' great competitors were men who knew their worth. It's said that when Donald Dinnie was asked to repeat his throw of the stone at Braemar because Queen Victoria had missed the original one, he responded by demanding, 'Two pounds, I'll no take a penny less.' He got it.

Dinnie was not the only man to affect such an attitude. Another of the all-time greats, George Clark from North Whitley, had not competed at the Aboyne games for fifteen years after the committee decided in 1934 to reduce all the prizes on offer by ten shillings. Clark threatened to lead a strike in protest and the committee were evidently so aggravated by what they called his 'insolence' that they suspended him for a year. Clark responded by writing such a rude letter to them that his ban was extended and he didn't return until 1951.

When it came to Dinnie, Queen Victoria would likely have paid the £2 herself, because it's fair to say Her Britannic Majesty had a bit of a soft spot for the 6-foot-tall athlete from

Aberdeenshire with the 15-inch biceps, the 48-inch chest and the bristling moustache. The Queen was not the only one to be smitten. 'He carried his sixteen stone of bone, flesh and muscle with an ease, grace and elasticity of motion rarely if indeed ever seen in a man of his proportions,' gushed the correspondent of the *North Star*. 'His dark, finely moulded features revealed intellectualism of the highest order ... his flashing penetrating eyes a sharp native wit.'

Dinnie was indeed a wonder of the Victorian Age, right up there with the steamship *Britannia* and Stephenson's Rocket. He has some claim to being the greatest all-round athlete of the nineteenth century and possibly the greatest Scottish athlete of all times. Born in 1836 at Balnacraig, close by where I was now standing watching a display of sword-dancing, Dinnie could sprint, hurdle, jump (long and high, possibly both at the same time) and pole-vault, as well as toss the caber, put the stone and throw the hammer. He was Highland Games champion for twenty straight years from 1856 to 1876. Oh, and he was also world wrestling champion. Perhaps his most remarkable feat was lifting two granite blocks with a combined weight of close to 750lbs and carrying them across a bridge near his parents' house in Kincardine O'Neil. The boulders – named Dinnie's Stones – are still there today. I'd had a look at them on my previous trip and I have to say that even considering thinking about lifting them had given me the feeling I had a hernia.

Dinnie – as his remark to the official who wanted the extra throw for Queen Victoria shows – had a real swagger to him. Often he was so confident of victory that he would toss the caber without bothering to take off his jacket. On other occasions he issued a challenge to beat any other man's two throws with one of his own. His arrogance seems to have been regarded with good grace by his competitors, though you can't help feeling one or two of them might have walked away muttering about sticking his caber somewhere impractical.

It's said that, during a fifty-year career, Dinnie won more than 11,000 events; his defeats were so rare they drew newspaper headlines around the world. Dinnie toured the globe – wrestling, throwing and sprinting in the USA, Canada, Australia and New Zealand. His travels were followed avidly by the Scottish newspapers and stories of his wondrous endeavours and narrow escapes – whether being run over by a pony and trap in Melbourne or struck with a flying hammer in Johannesburg – filled columns almost daily.

The *Manchester Echo* claimed that comparing other athletes to Dinnie was like 'comparing a bull mastiff to a half-starved terrier'. During his visit to the USA, the *Boston Herald* said that the best US athletes appeared diminutive when set beside him. In France, his escapades were compared favourably with those of Hercules, his strength with that of Samson.

Dinnie was said to have appeared before every European monarch. Along the way he earned around £25,000 (the equivalent of about £2 million today). Tragically, like many great athletes since, he invested it badly and, shortly before his death in 1916, he was reported to have been 'eking out a bare existence in Croydon', which seems a bitter and cruel fate for anybody.

The open Heavy Events at Aboyne commenced at 12.45 with the light hammer event, which was sponsored by an accountancy firm from Banchory. I took up a seat on the grass next to an enthusiastic family of four from New Hampshire, who announced themselves to be 'Scots on both sides'. The mother, who exuded the open-air wholesomeness of an L.L. Bean model, said they were over in Scotland exploring family roots. Like the Scots-Belgians, they identified whole-heartedly with the Highlands, although they had drawn the line at haggis. 'I mean, I guess if you were poor and all,' the father commented in explanation. 'But, you know, the Aberdeen Angus steaks are the best, right?' I told him that if he thought they were good he should try the steaks they got from Dexter cattle. I said they were the cattle the Highland crofters kept and they were so small they were no bigger than a Newfoundland dog and in winter they could bring them indoors. I said that Dexters were sweet-natured and had lovely furry ears and gleaming intelligent eyes. 'And the meat you get from them is really fantastic.' The father seemed eager, but from the look on his kids' faces, I could tell maybe they'd be keener to keep one as a pet than eat it.

The Americans were called Hunter – or at least their family had been at some point. They had come over for the Hunter clan gathering, which was held at Hunterston Castle in West Kilbride, possibly the only castle in the UK with a nuclear power station in the garden. I told them I had almost gone to the gathering myself because I had a feeling there might be a display of popinjay at it. Popinjay, unlike pretty much every other sport in this book, had never been banned. That was because it was the very thing the other sports had been banned to preserve – archery. Popinjay was also called vertical archery. It involved firing arrows at a target that was set high above your head. Since arrows come down as well as go up, this was by no means the safest way of shooting them, which may explain why popinjay had pretty died out of its own accord everywhere in the British Isles apart from one isolated pocket.

The people who had been slated to appear at Hunterston were the Ancient Society of Kilwinning Archers. Based at Kilwinning in Ayrshire, they had been founded sometime in the fifteenth century. The annual shooting match at Kilwinning Abbey had been held since 1488, making it one of the oldest sporting competitions in Britain, if not *the* oldest. The Kilwinning Abbey shoot had flourished during the days when bowmanship was compulsory and in the sixteenth century had so many entrants the competition had to be divided into categories based around age and social class. In 1830, the Ancient Society of Kilwinning Archers numbered around 300. They were sufficiently famous for King William IV to grant them the right to serve as his bodyguard whenever he visited Scotland. Later, Prince Albert the Royal Consort became the Society's patron and the archers afforded similar protection to Queen Victoria whenever she visited Ayrshire.

At Kilwinning, the cock bird which formed the most prized target was called a papingo, which was an old name for parrot. The papingo – which actually looked more like a pigeon – was a thing of some wonder and standing, and was originally carried to the tower on the top of the Burgh mace-bearer's civic Lochaber axe (a big two-handed thing that was said to be able to lop the heads off horses) in a procession that also featured the archers and a brass band. The archers marched along wearing splendid knitted tam o'shanters with a pom-pom in the centre and a ring around the inner rim that gave them the look of a target.

The actual targets – twenty-four chicks (worth one point each), four hens (three points) and the papingo (five points) – are mounted on a pole that juts out 10 or so feet from the tower of the abbey and 116 feet above the ground. The archers shoot at it with one foot on the front doorstep.

These are small targets and difficult to hit. In days of old, the competition could go on for many hours. Mind you, back then things weren't helped by the fact that the archers paused midway through the contest and processed around the town taking a drink in each of the pubs. Since Kilwinning had around twenty-five hostelries at that time, it can be imagined that the second half of the shoot was a good deal louder and less accurate than the first.

It was also a lot more dangerous. The shooting is done with old-fashioned long bows. Nowadays the arrows are rubber tipped which, since any that miss fall back down to earth at a velocity sufficient to split a skull, is a huge comfort to spectators. This was not always the case and the damage a real arrow can do can be seen on the gravestones in the church-yard. 'If it hit you in the head, well, it would come straight out of your bumhole,' one experienced archer I spoke to told me with no little relish.

The prize for victory at the Kilwinning shoot is the Silver Arrow dating from the 1720s. The trophy is festooned with medals that immortalise each year's winner, the exception being 1745. This is because the winner that year was Charles Boyd, a Jacobite who disappeared after the Battle of Culloden. Fearing that having an outlaw's name on the trophy might lead to it being confiscated by the Crown, the society left the medal blank, save for a tracery of what may be Jacobite roses. In 1793, the winner was an archer named David Boyle, a Scottish judge who sentenced the homicidal Edinburgh body-snatcher William Burke to be hanged. Other notable victors included an uncle and a cousin of Alexander Hamilton, the only signatory of the American Declaration of Independence to have his own rap musical.

Popinjay had once been popular all over Britain, but now only the event in Kilwinning and another one in Perthshire survived, though oddly the sport had remained highly popular in Belgium and the Netherlands where it was called staande-wip. I had watched various YouTube clips of competitions and it was plain that, particularly during contests between Belgium and the Netherlands (the two undisputed kings of popinjay), things could get pretty tense. In one international, a Flemish competitor's sturdily built mother charged on to congratulate

her lad after a brilliant shot and collided with him at such velocity he was flattened like a skittle by a cheese. He evidently failed
to recover from this dizzying collision and finished third. Quite
why this odd Scottish sport should have caught hold in the
Low Countries is a mystery. But then Belgians had embraced
other singular sports and it is worth remembering that the
nation still holds the Olympic title for live pigeon shooting –
a rifle equivalent of popinjay – thanks to the splendid efforts
of Leo de Lunden who killed twenty-one birds at the Paris
Games of 1900.

'Sounds like we should go to Kilwinning,' the American
dad said when I told him about popinjay. His wife nodded.
My daughter, who lives in Glasgow, had told me that the only
time she was in Kilwinning, she'd seen a drunk old man in
an Old Firm top fighting with a dog. But maybe that was
untypical, so I didn't mention it.

On the field at Aboyne, we'd moved on to the Throwing
28lb Weight by Ring contest, which was sponsored by a
joiner from a place with the pleasingly appropriate name of
Lumphanan. There was a lot of grunting and yelling. Many
of the competitors in the heavy events wore shorts beneath
their kilts. All had black vests advertising sponsor Glenfiddich.
For people of my generation, whose first encounter with the
Highland Games was the man on the Scott's Porage Oats
packet, this regalia was slightly disappointing.

After a pause for the High Leap Open, Men and Women
(best female £20, if more than two enter), we came to Geoff
Capes' specialism: Putting Heavy Stone Open. This was the

only Highland Heavy Event that had ever made the Olympics. Lifting rocks both one-handed and two-handed featured in the Olympics in 1896, 1904 and 1920, but for some reason chucking them had never caught on. A stone-throwing event had taken place in St Louis in 1904, but that competition took place – alongside bolo-hurling, mud-fighting and shimmying up the greasy pole – on the so-called 'Anthropological Days' when sports were undertaken by the Pygmies, Patagonians and the other unfortunate indigenous peoples who'd been corralled into the exhibits at the nearby World's Fair. In 1906, those who felt the Games should return regularly to its historic birthplace organised an unofficial Olympics in Athens and the stone throw made its one and only appearance in the real Games. Nikolaos Georgantas of Greece threw the 6.4kg stone an amazing 19.92 metres to defeat the legendary Martin Sheridan, a New York police officer who was known as the Irish Whale. I might have related all this to the New England family, but after I told them about Capes and his budgies, they remembered that they might have left the oven on in their motorhome and had gone to check.

There was something simple and easy to grasp about the heavy events, the setting was hard to beat and the crowd was cheerful and free from partisanship, apparently happy just to be there, and after the previous two years who could blame them?

Though there was great excitement about the throwing of stones and cabers, for me the best event of the day for spectacle was the 56lb Weight Over the Bar, which saw the big men attempting to loft the mighty weight over what looked like a reasonably high set-up for a pole vault. I read later that the task was sometimes likened to trying to hoick a small child over a double-decker bus, though you have to wonder what social services would make of that, even in Glasgow.

After the weight throw was done, the Tug O' War began. I wandered off to have a look at Strachans of Royal Deeside, a shop that had a greatest choice of oatcakes that I have ever seen (and I'm a big fan of oatcakes) and then caught the bus back to Aberdeen, the infernal thwacking of the bus roof a minor inconvenience after an uplifting day, in a lovely place and a night with a trouser press still to come.

12

An Uncommon Bias

CROWN GREEN BOWLING, LANCASHIRE

One of my former neighbours had been a semi-pro footballer in his youth. 'When I had to give it up, I took to bowls,' he said. 'Went all over the country playing, up to the Highlands of Scotland, everywhere.'

'Was that crown green bowling, then?' I asked.

My neighbour pulled the sort of face you might imagine Liz Truss (remember her?) making if you suggested she increase the upper tax bracket by 25 per cent, use the money to renationalise the railways and then celebrate by taking ecstasy and having a three-in-a-bed romp with Emmanuel Macron and Angela Merkel.

'Oh no,' he said, with what was as near as a retired Durham miner could come to a pout. 'I wouldn't have had anything to do with that.'

Crown green bowling, you see, is bowls like it used to

be before middle-class Victorians like W. G. Grace – who dominated greens almost as much as he did cricket fields – tamed it and turned it into the stuff of drawing-room comedy. Lawn bowls was tea and cucumber sandwiches, crown green bowling was pork pie and a pint of mild. More than that, it was a bookie's dream with huge money wagered not only on the outcomes of matches, but of individual woods. In lawn bowls, the amateur star might take home a silver sugar basin. In crown green, he carried off a big envelope stuffed with cash, sometimes even if he lost. Because while betting against yourself might seem wrong to outsiders, a professional businessman has to take out insurance against failure, doesn't he? Crown green was as dangerous and flashy as bowls can get. If Fast Eddie Felson from *The Hustler* had played bowls, crown green would have been his game.

Crown green is different from lawn bowls in other ways too, of course. The greens are not flat, but slope away from the central ridge or hill, the jack has a bias like the woods and the whole green is used for a single game rather than being split into strip-like 'rinks' so that multiple matches can be played at the same time. Like golf courses, crown greens have their own characters. At Llandudno Oval, the green is an immense 45 yards square with four humps rather than a single crown. Dewsbury is treacherous and noted for its strange hollows. The green at Weaverham in Cheshire has the highest crown of any ground in England, while Shotton in Flintshire is infamous for the speed of its downhill slope. Some lawn bowls players see this aspect of crown green as proof that it is more or less a lottery, like playing snooker on a wobbly table. Crown green players sneer back that lawn bowls is nothing more than 'finger billiards' that demands no more physical effort than feeding a goldfish. The gap between the two games seems small to outsiders, but Europe was left devastated by disputes over far slighter and more arcane differences. The ridge in a square of grass is the sporting equivalent of transubstantiation. It doesn't seem much to most people, but it is, almost literally, a hill bowlers would die on.

I'd been to watch crown green bowls a decade or so ago when the cricket match I'd been aiming to see in the Bolton Association, or possibly the Bolton League (and at that point the animosity between those two rivals made the ruckus between crown and lawn bowls looks like a teenage lovers' tiff), had been rained off. The game was a panel match at the Red Lion in Westhoughton. The panel had been formed at the pub in October 1908 and back then it went by the more formal name of the Lancashire Professional Bowling Association. Originally there were around ten pubs in the Bolton and Wigan area that hosted panel matches and the LPBA had more than 600 members. Most of the players and spectators were miners and the games were timed to start just after the finish of the early shift.

When the panel was formed, some of the bowlers in it were earning around £750 a year, close to three times what professional footballers were taking home at that point. They took their fees as a percentage of the gate receipts – and four-figure crowds were common. To this sum was added prize money.

Not factored into their earnings were side bets, which were frequent and often enormous. Before the First World War and after it, the panel bowlers were among the highest-paid sportsmen in Britain.

In the late 1960s, it appeared that the panel bowlers had hit the big time once again when the BBC started its own televised tournament *Top Crown* (the bowls equivalent of the snooker show *Pot Black* and trial-biking contest *Kick Start*). Featuring members of the panel dressed in matching pastel-coloured jumpers and caps, the show had commentary by Harry Rigby – generally regarded as the Eddie Waring of the woods – whose nasal Mancunian accent gave his cries of 'Has it enough? Has it enough?' and 'They're cobbing their bowls here!' the tone of a John Cooper Clarke poem. Expert punditry was supplied by *Z Cars* actor Colin Welland. The show ran for close to two decades before the BBC lost interest. The inimitable Rigby went back to covering sport for the *Stockport News*, while Welland had to content himself with writing the Oscar-winning screenplay for *Chariots of Fire*, Scipio Musabini and all.

These days the panel has been whittled down to a select group of twenty-four bowlers who play each other at the Red Lion every weekday afternoon of the year. The weather means nothing to them. They carry on through pouring rain. If it snows, they brush it off the turf and if it's foggy, they wear head torches. Rain that had driven the cricket-ers into the pavilion and Aunt Sally players to the pub bar meant nothing to these blokes; they'd have regarded the onset of a nuclear winter as a poor excuse not to get on with the game.

The match I saw was leisurely. There was clearly betting but it was very makeshift, done by men with notebooks and pencils. There was a furtive air to it, which was not all that surprising as I later learned that, strictly speaking (and how else do His Majesty's Revenue and Customs talk?), it was illegal. My main memory of the afternoon was of the two old men sitting near me who spoke in Lancashire accents as crumbly as cheese and kept up a stream of chatter throughout, not much of it with any relationship to what was going on in front of them. At one point they discussed a near-death experience. 'I heard this ruddy great crash about midnight,' the first one said. 'And when I looked out of the window, there was this block of ice about 2-foot square sat right in the middle of the lawn. You know what it was? Effluent from an aircraft toilet, that's bloomin' what. Falls down through the air and freezes, apparently. Imagine If I'd been stood out there. I'd have been killed by a block of frozen sewage. What would my grandchildren have said to that, eh?'

His companion thought for a moment. 'It was how he'd have wanted to go?' he replied.

I laughed so loud beer shot out of my nose. If you're a writer looking for jokes, Bolton is a great place to go. The people are warm and friendly and they pretty much do your job for you.

The great schism in bowls occurred in the Victorian era. Before that, the game seemed moored not so much in a slough of despond as in an entire urban Berkshire of despair. It is a game with ancient origins. The name bowls derives from the Latin for bubble. Herodotus claimed it was invented by the Lydians in what is now western Turkey as a means of distracting themselves from hunger during a terrible famine. England's first green was laid in Southampton during the reign of Edward I. But a century later, Edward III, fearful that the manly pursuit of archery was being undermined, ordered the prohibition of all 'stone, wood and iron throwing under penalty of imprisonment'.

Henry VIII took a similar stance. In 1541, he blamed the desperate state of the archery trade (bowyers, fletchers, stringers and arrowhead-makers all wandering the streets looking for work) on the 'customable usage' of bowls. The ban on bowls was very specifically applied to tradesmen, craftsmen, journeymen and the like, which was lucky as Henry himself was a very keen bowls player (he reputedly used a cannon-ball) but didn't belong to any of those groups. Henry's statute bizarrely remained in place until it was repealed in 1845, meaning any member of the working class playing bowls before then was effectively an outlaw.

While the lower orders were denied their bowling rights, the upper classes continued to play enthusiastically. In 1552, the bias in the bowling wood was invented by Charles Brandon, Duke of Suffolk, while apparently in the middle of eloping to Spain with the king's sister. It was largely an accident (the invention of the wobbly bowl, not the elopement). The bowl Brandon was using smashed in half. In a rush to finish his match he fixed it quickly using wood cut from the banister-rail of a widow named Mary Woodhall – imagine the look on her face when she found out what he'd done. The banister wood was heavier than that of the original half and so the ball curled as it rolled. The sight of Brandon's ball curving around opposing woods was inspirational and other players began to copy it. At first the level of bias in the bowl was a matter of personal preference. Some bowls were more biased than others and so were the players, as the old joke has it. In Victorian times, bias was standardised. The move was helped by the invention, in 1890, of a machine that calibrated the exact bias on bowls with complete accuracy. The machine was the creation of a man from Edinburgh named Taylor. When Taylor teamed up with commercial bowls-maker Frank Rolph, his brilliant invention was brought south and installed in a factory at Penshurst in Kent where it was as carefully guarded as the Enigma machine was at Bletchley during the Second World War. The wood used to make bowls was the ubiquitous lignum vitae. When this was replaced by phenol formaldehyde, a prolonged argument ensued over whether woods should still be called woods – though only between people with too much time on their hands, obviously.

King Charles I had as unhappy a relationship with bowls as he did with Parliament. Playing a match at Barking Hall in Essex, the home of the wealthy Richard Shute, the king reputedly lost £1,000 in a single session, though thankfully he turned down Shute's invitation to carry on playing in case his luck changed, saying that he had a wife and children to consider.

Gambling on the outcome was arguably the most prodigious of that on any English sport, including horse racing. Entire family estates were rolled away on bowling greens. In 1648, it is said that Sir Edward Hungerford gambled his house on a match and while watching his last wood curl hopelessly away from the jack remarked with a heavy sigh, 'There goes Rowden'. Sir John Suckling, the inventor of cribbage and friend of Robert Dover, gambled so mightily on bowls it is said his sisters would be seen weeping beside the green in fear that he was about to send them into penury. Little wonder that the Bishop of Worcester, tutor to the future King Charles II, said that bowls was celebrated for three things wasted: 'time, money and curses'.

The Restoration saw a mad explosion in bowls playing. Despite his old teacher's warning, Charles II was as big a fan of bowling as his father had been. He even issued a set of rules, one of which prohibited men from wearing high-heeled shoes on the green – not a problem they likely ever had to deal with in Westhoughton.

Then, for no reason anyone can fathom, after the accession of Queen Anne, bowls entered a period of stagnation that lasted close to 150 years. Prohibitions on gambling issued in the reign of George II did not help, but otherwise it is hard to see why the game fell from popularity. By the mid-nineteenth century, bowls was an endangered sport. The *Field* reported in the 1860s that 'by degrees many of the old greens have vanished . . . Today we find comparatively few greens within easy reach of London and we may perhaps regret that the game has to some extent fallen into desuetude.'

It was the Scots who saved bowls and made it respectable again – in particular one Scot, William Mitchell from Kilmarnock, who had begun playing the game as an eleven-year-old in 1814. When Mitchell started out, bowls was, by his own account, a sport enjoyed mainly in the countryside by a few elderly gentlemen of independent means. By the time Mitchell had finished, there were more than 10,000 committed bowlers in Scotland alone.

Around 1848, after meetings with all the bowls clubs of Scotland, Mitchell helped establish a uniform code of laws regulating the game. Over the next thirty years, these would become the standard laws throughout the British Empire. The Scottish Bowling Association was created a few years after Mitchell's death in 1884 and became to bowls what the Royal and Ancient was to golf, the MCC to cricket and the NDA to darts.

Under Mitchell's watchful and, one suspects, Presbyterian eye, bowls matches were played for formal prizes rather than for stake money. One of the first great bowling competitions of the Victorian era was held in Kirkcudbright in 1864. It attracted close to 300 entrants. First-placed William Currie from Troon won a tea service, while the second-placed bowler received 'a handsome French timepiece'. There was no gambling, and drinking was kept to a minimum, for as Mitchell noted, great care was required to prevent such occasions 'degenerating and making an opening for the censorious'.

At this point, bowls, like cricket, was being viewed by Christian groups and temperance societies as a means of luring blokes out of pubs and into the fresh air. By 1894, there were hundreds of new bowling clubs in England, each with its own green and a pavilion. The new bowls clubs required space and land and so bowls became associated not with the crowded inner cities but with the suburbs and with market towns and villages. The atmosphere had changed. A game that had once been a byword for unruliness had been tamed. It was now more akin to lawn tennis than cock fighting.

The man who helped re-popularise bowls in England and Wales was one of the most recognisable sporting figures of the Victorian, or indeed any, age: W. G. Grace. The good doctor had been arguably sport's first true superstar when playing cricket for Gloucestershire and England, his vast size, flowing beard and brilliance with both bat and ball propelling him to the height of fame. By 1899, his skills were beginning to fail and he left Gloucestershire for London where he was appointed to manage cricket and other games at the Crystal Palace. He was over fifty by then and had slowed down considerably. One day, Grace spotted bowls being played on the beautiful green at the palace and he quickly took up the game up with his usual competitive fury. Soon he was good enough to be captain of the England team and lead them in what would be the first bowls international, against Scotland in 1903. He continued playing for England for the next five years. Grace, I should add, also played billiards and curling, but rejected calls to take up lawn tennis, which he evidently regarded as a little too effete for a man of his gargantuan muscular manliness.

After the First World War, lawn bowls entered a golden era of amateurism, predominantly played by middle-aged men in spruce private clubs. It was said by the gentlemen who ran lawn bowls that that professionalism could 'find no opportunity' in the sport. The attitude against professionalism was summarised by Humphrey Dingley in 1893: 'If money prizes continue to be the rule at public tournaments love for the game may develop into a sordid hunt after "filthy lucre".' He suggested that a more fitting prize would be a trophy, such as a pipe, matchbox or 'lordly vase of high artistic excellence' – which would have come in handy for a pitman. Furthermore, as E. T. Ayers noted in 1894, the heavy gambling 'in Lancashire and the northern parts of England' was likely to drive away 'the quieter sort of company' depriving them of exercise and the opportunity for 'kindly social intercourse'. Lawn bowls players and supporters doubtless said a respectful 'Hear, hear' to that. Their confidence in the primacy of the amateur game was, however, misplaced. Back in the spots where bowls had originally thrived, by the side and round the back of pubs, a very different game was gathering a large and vociferous audience all of its own.

The rejuvenation of crown green bowling had occurred almost in parallel to that of the game's genteel rival. The repeal of Henry VIII's law and an increasing number of clubs clamouring for business saw a boom in the laying of bowling greens, that was encouraged by the invention of the motor mower (before that greens were cut by experts with scythes who, according *The Field*, were in short supply and charged a fortune – a bit like plumbers today). By the 1870s, crown green bowling was well-established as a professional sport with newspapers – particularly regional titles in the Midlands and north-west England – carrying full reports on key matches, which during the summer occurred almost daily.

In 1873, the annual Talbot Handicap was held at the Talbot Hotel in Blackpool and that was soon followed by an even more prestigious event, the Waterloo Handicap at the nearby Waterloo Hotel. These two events swiftly became so popular – attracting over 1,000 entrants apiece – it was said that they extended the seaside resort's holiday season by a full month. Not that winter put a stop to crown green bowling. There were outdoor competitions held even at Christmas when, according to the bowls writer George Burrows, 'a frozen green rattled louder than do the boards at Alexandra Palace' and the fog was so dense the jack could not be seen when it was 25 yards away.

The men bet on themselves, settling odds, by Burrows' account, 'in the street, in boarding houses, in tramcars'. The gambling on the Blackpool handicaps went on all over the country with bookmakers willingly laying odds on outsiders of upwards of 500–1. Burrows spoke to one pitman who had entered the competition and put a pound on himself to win at 1,000–1. His hopes mounted as he progressed through the competition until finally, after close to six weeks of competition, he went out a couple of rounds before the final with what would have been a life-changing victory within his grasp.

The Waterloo attracted such vast crowds that stewards had to be on hand to prevent spectators encroaching on the green. People watched from the windows of the nearby boarding houses and from the rooftops too. There was a grandstand for those who could afford it, while the sixpence standing entrants were lined up ten deep around the green. The green itself was immense, 45 yards square. The turf had been cut, like that of hundreds of bowling greens across the country, from the English side of the Solway, the great flat tidal plain around Burgh by Sands and Silloth. The marsh was flat and windswept, the turf traditionally cut in December and January, peeled from the earth like the skin of some vast beast. The geese and wading birds that over-wintered on the Solway Firth greeted the arrival of the cutters with a chorus of honking protest.

Lawn bowls was played in private clubs where the only spectators were usually the players' families. Even when crowds assembled for big competitions such as the national championships, they watched in a hushed and priestly silence. The rules of lawn bowls also governed the behaviour of the crowd, who were expected to maintain a position of neutrality throughout matches. Even a call of 'Well done!' from a spectator after a successful shot was regarded by umpires and players as an offence tantamount to farting in front of the pope.

Crowds at crown green bowls were very different. They were more like those that watched cricket at Bramall Lane and Old Trafford. There were yells of encouragement, wise cracks and catcalls. Playing in front of large partisan crowds imposed greater pressure on the players. The bookmakers knew that; it was why they offered such phenomenal odds against amateur players. Winning at Blackpool required nerves of reinforced concrete and the single-minded focus of Sam Matterface in pursuit of a dodgy metaphor. Like all real gamblers, the crown green bowlers needed to be able to shut out not only the noise, but also the thought of what winning might mean to them.

Even smaller competitions at pubs that attracted the semi-pros would charge one shilling admission to competitors and hand out £2 along with – a singular detail – a copper kettle as a prize. Most of the ties were played for threepence a side.

Burrows saw crown green as the bastion of blue-collar workers. 'The strict amateur in industrial England is of the middle class,' he wrote. 'The professional and semi-professional is the collier, factory hand and other horny-handed son of toil.' The competitors wore clogs, flat caps and mufflers. They swore in rage when they lost and jigged with joy when they won.

One of the greatest Victorian crown green pros was Tom Taylor, who went by the lyrical nickname of 'Owd Toss'. When a journalist and keen amateur player approached him asking for a match, Taylor first asked him if he took his coat off when he played, then if he took his waistcoat off and finally if he removed the starched collar of his shirt. Because only a man who did so was, by Taylor's reckoning, a real player. You couldn't send down a wood wearing a blazer.

Taylor was part of a cluster of tough full-time pros that included men such as John Peace, Gerard Hart, George Beattie and Dan Greenhalgh. They played in matches for thousands of pounds in stake money and hundreds more in side bets. Most had begun their working lives as pitmen or cotton mill workers, building up savings from tanner bets on matches held behind village pubs until they had enough to quit their day jobs. They were proud craftsmen who looked on amateurs with the sharp scorn a jobbing electrician has for the DIY dabbler with smouldering eyebrows. They delighted in stuffing any well-spoken chap in a straw hat who ventured onto their turf.

Crown green maintained its independence and flourished. The Waterloo had carried on during both world wars (one of the winners during the second conflict was the brilliantly named Yorkshireman Tedber Tinker) and it was shown live on television in the 1970s and '80s, attracting more than 2,000 entrants. The Waterloo Hotel in Blackpool was often called the 'Wembley of Bowls'. This was true, though it was a good deal easier to get to, and the beer was better and much cheaper. The pub first opened its doors in 1901. It was a big brick Victorian place of the kind you will see standing at major road junctions or on the fringes of towns all over the country. Behind the pub was a fantastic arena with stands and terraces that hold 4,500 people. Unhappily, in recent years the pub's owners have gone bust, after crowds had fallen and TV coverage had ended. The hotel took on a neglected and mildewed air. COVID did the rest. The famous stadium was now in such a state of disrepair it could no longer host the event and so I found myself heading across Blackpool to Fleetwood Bowling Club, the new venue for the Waterloo.

I was still slightly dizzy from the train journey over from Preston. That had been on a tiny train that was so packed it was a wonder the rivets didn't pop from the panelling. I was also the only man on board who wasn't either wearing a PVC nurse's outfit and false breasts, or dressed as 1970s tennis ace Chrissie Evert. That I was sober further marked me out as a crazy freak.

Despite the drunken jollity, Blackpool had a lugubrious atmosphere. It was a place where modern Britain and the country I had grown up in collided. One minute you were looking at a gaudy poster for a transvestite extravaganza, the next at the blacked-out windows of the private shop with its printed signs offering 'marital aids'. Hen parties in pink Stetsons and printed T-shirts reading 'Sperm Donors Wanted' staggered whoopingly past old men and women, who looked like they were on their way to a fancy dress party kitted out as Albert Tatlock and Ena Sharples.

When I was a kid, my parents had brought me here every year to see the Blackpool Illuminations. I recall it as one of the high points of my early life, but when I mention it to my mum these days, she rolls her eyes and says, 'Thank God I'll never have to do that again.' Walking along the Golden Mile,

I understood what she meant. There was something a bit unsettling about all the kiss-me-quick merriment. Blackpool seemed to be permanently hovering on the cusp of a hangover or a punch-up.

Fleetwood Bowling Club was mercifully free from fancy dress, unless you counted the blazer of the bloke sitting three rows along from me, which looked like he'd stolen it from a horse. Behind me, three chaps from Wigan kept up a constant commentary on the play ('He'd not sweat in a sauna, this lad', 'That's the prettiest wood I've seen since *West Side Story*') while lamenting the poor quality of the local pies.

The games went along in a slow and determined way. The most arresting thing to the untutored eye was the way the players ran after their wood, executing a series of elaborate skips, jumps and sashays around it, presumably in the hope that the vibrations would drive it in the direction they required. The most famous exponent of this peculiar routine was Vernon 'The Dancing Major' Lee, who cavorted across the grass like he'd been let loose from the floor of Wigan Casino. Crown green has a strict 'no stamping rule' and occasionally the referee would have to admonish the over-enthusiastic high stepper, or even disqualify a wood. The latter had famously occurred in the doubles final of BBC's *Top Crown* in 1982, provoking Harry Rigby to proclaim, 'That is the most expensive stamp since the Penny Black!'

The old Waterloo Hotel had been the scene of some of the most celebrated crown green matches in history. In 1911, the final between Fred Threlfall and Tommy Meadows saw the final two woods lying so close to the jack that a piece of straw (the equivalent of quoits' ten-pound note) had to be used to determine which was closest. Meadows celebrated prematurely, but Threlfall won.

Crown green was a game that – like darts – nurtured and celebrated eccentrics. The 1961 Waterloo Handicap final featured seventy-one-year-old Charles Taylor, known to everyone as Charlie the Lion Tamer because he'd worked for years as an assistant at Blackpool's zoo. His opponent was the semi-legendary John 'The Feather' Featherstone, a publican from Leigh. The Feather was a battle-hardened pro, whereas The Lion Tamer had only begun playing in his fifties and had never reached such rarefied heights before. The impression of a hapless novice was exacerbated by the fact that he insisted on playing in a black beret and wire-rimmed spectacles. Small and skinny, he looked like Charles Hawtrey on a French holiday. The Feather was big and gruff, the sort of publican who'd scowl and point at the clock if anyone had the temerity to ask for a drink thirty seconds after closing time. He quickly rumbled into the lead. The Lion Tamer fought back gamely. In a hushed and silent atmosphere, the game rested at 20 apiece when the final woods were bowled. The Feather got the better of it and The Lion Tamer was done.

Another famous figure was Old Bill Lacy from Wigan, who began his sporting and gambling life as a greyhound trainer in London and took up bowls only after he'd retired. In 1957, he won the Waterloo Handicap, having also progressed to the quarter-finals of Blackpool's other great contest, the Talbot

Trophy (the Talbot Hotel had been demolished in the 1960s; the famous bowling green is now a car park – feel free to boo at this point). As far as anyone knew, nobody had ever done 'the double' and thousands turned up to watch the match between Lacy and the splendidly monikered Wally Fish (a tool fitter at Leyland Motors), with touts outside offering half-crown tickets for £1 a pop. In a hard-fought match, Lacy, fortified by regular swigs from a flask of tea, eventually triumphed. He made it through to the final by defeating Paul Rocroft from Liverpool in the semis. By now, the aged bowler was tired and prepared for the final that evening by having a long nap. His opponent was a man named Johnny Ball, who also came from Wigan. The game was nip and tuck; with 21 needed to win the two men were tied at 17 apiece. But weariness overcame Lacy and he lost the final points, finally shaking hands with his opponent and saying, 'Well, at least Wigan won it . . .'

It was a sentiment the blokes behind me would doubtless have echoed, though unfortunately for them the only two bowlers from Wigan who'd made it through to the last 64 had been knocked out long before the finals. The winner was Paul Dudley from Radcliffe, near Manchester.

By then I'd wandered off in search of food. I had a decent meal in a restaurant back in Blackpool. The place was busy, but I noticed that there was a sign saying it was shutting for good the following Saturday. I asked the restaurant-owner why he was closing down. He was a small man with the sort of ingrained, melancholic expression that suggested a Tammy

Wynette ballad was playing on a loop in his subconscious. He said he had come to Britain from Latin America twelve years before and everything had been great. 'But now, you look around, prices going up, up, up – fuel, raw materials, electricity, gas . . . You can no longer make a living and everything is falling apart. But what bothers me most here, it is the passivity of the people. All the time things are going from worse to worse, but nobody does anything. In China, Iran, even in my country, people are out on the streets protesting. Here people say, "Yes, it is terrible," then they shrug their shoulders and go to the pub to watch football.' His eyes drooped like those of a bloodhound and he shook his head. 'I will close down and go back home. It is better there, for me.'

I wished him well and walked out onto the seaside streets. Darkness had fallen. On the Golden Mile, a man dressed as a nun was playing a game of knock-up cricket with Spiderman and a penguin, using a cardboard cut-out of Gareth Southgate as a wicket and a 3-foot-long pink inflatable penis as a bat. During the first COVID lockdown, people had said that life in Britain would never be the same again. It was reassuring to see that, in Blackpool at least, things had returned completely to normal.

13

Bullets and Bruised Shins

ROAD BOWLING, COUNTY ARMAGH

The start-line was chalked on a tarmac road that squirmed its way between fields so verdantly green you practically needed sunglasses to look at them. Yellow council signs warned 'Caution Road Bowls Ahead Prepare to Stop', which must have been baffling to any unwitting visitor to County Armagh. The crowd bubbled and flowed along the verges, filling the air with throaty cries of encouragement and outrage and the occasional cloud of vape smoke. Tension buzzed in the air like wasps above a picnic. In front of me, a man in a multi-pocketed shooting vest collected wads of notes from frantic betting men in warm-up coats, licking his pencil before scribbling names on what looked like an old-fashioned waiter's notepad. There was an air of carnival excitement around the place that would have sent a shiver down the spine of a mountain range.

Part of the reason for that was the emergence onto the road of Armagh's greatest bowler, Thomas Mackle from Clonmain. Tall and rangy, with a wild mop of dark hair, bristling beard and laughter-lined eyes, Mackle was Hollywood central casting's idea of an Irishman. If he'd appeared in a US film, his entrance would have been marked by jaunty fiddle music.

Mackle comes from a family of road bowlers. 'My grandfather threw, my aunts and uncles, my mother and my daddy.' He worked on the family farm. For a time, his great rival had been Cathal Toal. Toal took a modern approach to training, working out in a gym, doing stretching exercises and talking about the dynamics of the sport. Mackle was unimpressed, commenting he would never set foot in a gym. He keeps fit, he says, by chasing sheep and built up his muscles lifting calves and wrangling cattle. It clearly worked. Mackle is a superstar of the sport, sucking up titles as a great blue whale does krill. He won his first senior All-Ireland Championship in 2016 and carried off the King of the Road title four times on the trot. He has a self-confidence that has a few critics wondering if it isn't a synonym for arrogance.

I was standing on a grass verge just outside Newtownhamilton, a village of 3,000 people that is the epicentre of road bowling in County Armagh. In the past, the bowlers from the north have generally taken second place to their competitors from Cork, the sport's great stronghold in the republic. However, a surge in interest and a well-organised youth policy started to tilt the balance in favour of the northern county. Arguably the greatest female bowler of all time, Kelly Mallon, came from Armagh. She recently supplanted Cork's Gretta Cormican as the woman with the most All-Ireland titles and she is still only in her twenties. Today, the men's All Ireland final would pit a home bowler against a rival from the south: Mackle, the Ulster champion, against Michael Bohane, a Garda from Cork, who had recently been crowned champion of Munster.

Road bowling was reputedly invented in Ireland in the late seventeenth century by the soldiers of King William of Orange, who alleviated their boredom while besieging Jacobite strongholds by throwing cannonballs around. Since a similar sport called klootscheiten – moors bowling – is still popular in the Netherlands (Dutch moors bowlers, including champion Silke 'The Flying Dutchwoman' Tulk, are regulars on the Irish roads), this has a certain sense to it.

Despite its military origins, the British government banned the sport for more than 200 years, claiming it was not only dangerous but 'revolutionary'. Luckily nobody in Ireland seemed to pay much attention and the game thrived in Cork and Armagh in particular. Here the great names from the past – Michael McCarthy Quirke, Buck McGrath, Scotty Leonard, Red Crowley – trip off the tongues of bowling aficionados as easily as those of the 1966 World Cup-winning team spill from the mouths of English football fans.

The projectile used in road bowling is still a cannonball pretty much, possibly like the one Henry VIII allegedly used to play skittles. Made of iron, it measures a little less than 8 inches in circumference and weighs about 28 ounces; by way of comparison, a cricket ball, which is roughly the same size, weighs a little less than 6 ounces. In Armagh, they call it a 'bullet'.

The aim of the sport is simple: to get to the finish line in the fewest number of throws. Two or more bowlers compete in the match, which is also called a 'score' – a remnant of the days when competitors had twenty throws each and whoever got furthest won. If two or more bowlers take the same number of throws to get to the finish line, then the ball that crosses it by the furthest margin is the winner.

The thrower has a couple of helpers. The 'shower' is there for wise counsel on the best line to throw. A second helper runs up ahead following the line that has been decided on. After each throw a mark is made on the road where the ball landed, even if it lands on the grass verge. The next throw is taken from that mark. Sometimes, in order to cut a corner, or to avoid the long grass at a road junction, the bowler lofts the ball in the air. This is quite a danger for spectators and the warning signs along the road are best heeded unless you are wearing shinpads and a crash helmet.

The routes taken by road bowlers were established long ago and were often drawn by hand with key places – gates, tall trees, corners – marked on them as on a pirate's treasure map. The course in today's final ran up the incline of Garvey's Brae, across the high meadow, past the 'mushroom houses' and towards Chandler's Cross.

The local favourite Mackel's presence and style was dramatic. He took a thirty-pace run to the mark, leaping into the air in his delivery stride and wind-milling his bowling arm round in a whirling blur. It might have looked brutal and uncontrolled, but in fact Mackel was noted for the accuracy of his throwing. Watching him made me think of the similarly theatrical – and similarly dark-haired – Australian fast bowler Dennis Lillee.

Mackel's opponent, Michael Bohane, took an early lead. There had been talk that in recent years Mackel had lost some of his spark, but he regained a piece of it now in front of his home fans and struck back with his third throw. I followed along behind. True fans get on ahead of the bowlers, but that struck me as something you could only do if you were nimble, clear-sighted and had a good idea what was going on, none of which applied to me. The bowling ball is made of what the Pathé News commentator called 'crude iron' and travels at around 60mph. Shortly before the match began, I had asked the man standing next to me, who was wearing an impressive gabardine coat and carrying a walking stick, if people ever got hit by the bowl. 'Well,' he replied cheerily, 'if any of them do, they'll surely deserve it.' Subsequently, I had a vision of myself felled by a savage crack to the knee and surrounded by angry people whose wager I had just buggered up with my idiocy.

From a perch on a high verge, I watched the ballet of Bohane and Mackel's coaches as they placed themselves in the road to mark the best path ahead. They stood with their feet wide apart and crouched frog-like on the tarmac. When the ball sped past, they'd raise one foot and twist their bodies round to follow its progress. It looked like they were engaged in a Gaelic form of Tai Chi.

Bohane had a more economical, less flamboyant style than his rival. His run began with a series of stuttering steps before he moved into top gear over four or five paces and unleashed the ball with a whipping arm. Somewhere in the back of my mind was the idea that, at one point in the 1980s, cerebral Middlesex and England cricket captain Mike Brearley had witnessed Irish road bowling and concluded that some of the players might come in handy at cricket, delivering a ball underarm at the sort of cracking pace attributed to Georgian fast bowlers such as David Harris, who terrorised opposing batsmen for a decade in the late eighteenth century until he was forced to retire due to severe gout. Brearley, in my memory, had brought a couple of bowlers to the nets and the results had been impressive. Sadly, nothing came of it, despite the interest of the England skipper. Brearley, I should say, had long been intrigued by the possibilities of under-arm bowling and had even bowled it himself, notably to Leicestershire's infamously belligerent Rhodesian all-rounder Brian Davidson. Davidson had been so enraged by the sight of the ball being lobbed towards him in this unlikely fashion that he'd threatened to punch the Middlesex skipper in the face if he continued. It seemed unlikely that even the pugnacious Davidson would have taken a similar line with Bohane or Mackel and watching the 'bullet' thundering from their hands, I could see that Brearley had a point. They'd make a useful addition to any T20 side.

Bohane fought his way back into the lead, to the dismay of the locals, but Mackel wasn't done. When a van found its way through the stewards in their high-vis jackets and lurched onto the course halfway down Mackel's run-up, he simply charged around it and, throwing with renewed fury, overtook Bohane once again. He held onto the lead comfortably enough after that, his bowl rolling across the finish line first to roars of approval.

Mackel was plainly delighted. And why wouldn't he be? He'd just scooped the first prize of €5,575, never mind what he might have earned by way of side bets. That was a big prize for road bowling, but money was on offer everywhere; even small events had prizes of €200 to the winner. Bohane himself had recently been involved in a €2,000-a-side match with Seamus Sexton.

While spectators scrummaged their ways into the crowded pubs and bars of Newtownhamilton, I walked away to find the car with the friend I was staying with. There was a burble of excited conversation all around. Mackel was a local idol, but I was pleased that an elderly bloke to my left, whose face was so reddened by sun and wind he looked to be fashioned from pantiles, commented to nobody in particular that while the young fellow was a fine player, sure enough, he'd have been no match for Mick Barry.

Nobody around offered to disagree, which was hardly surprising since Mick Barry was to road bowling what the Belgian Eddy Merckx was to professional cycling and Australia's Sir Donald Bradman was to batting. He was pure and simply The King of the Road. Songs were written about him.

Barry came from the village of Waterfall outside Cork city and spoke with an accent so soft and mellifluous it was practically a whistle. The head gardener at University College, Barry was as strong as a horse and as light on his feet as a ballroom dancer. He'd become obsessed with bowling as a boy, almost to the exclusion of everything else. Despite the fact his mother discouraged him for fear bowling would lead him inevitably into a life of beer and gambling, he practised like a fanatic.

Barry's style was compact, yet explosive. While most men before him had bowled in trousers and a shirt, he donned shorts and a vest. It was a signal that he was a true athlete not just some fellow who'd stepped out of the saloon bar after half a dozen pints.

The Cork gardener won eleven titles in the Republic of Ireland and, when the All-Ireland Championship was inaugurated in 1963, dominated that competition too, claiming eight titles between 1965 and 1975, even though he was by then middle-aged. Barry's most celebrated feat came in 1955 when he had achieved what had previously seemed impossible, lofting his 'cannonball' over the 90-foot-high Chetwynd Viaduct. On another memorable occasion, he hurled his 28-ounce ball straight over Mary Anne's pub on Dublin Hill to wrestle back the advantage in a tight contest.

Despite his mother's fears, Barry neither smoked nor drank.

His abstinence contributed to his longevity – he eventually retired from the sport aged seventy-eight.

Like quoits, road bowling has enjoyed an unexpected rise in popularity over the past three decades. It has spread out into Wexford and Kerry where, according to the *Dublin Evening Herald*, it is particularly popular with teenage girls – generally a group that takes the same enthusiastic delight in sport as they do in their fathers' jokes. By 1996, there were so many new people taking up the road bowling that the sport's governing body, Bol-Chumann na hÉireann, produced a little booklet called 'Splitting the Sop', designed to teach newcomers the rules and basics of the sport. One of the things it told them was, of course, that a sop is a bunch of grass placed as a target by the bowler's assistants and splitting it is the equivalent of hitting the bullseye.

Surprisingly, there was no road bowling in England, Scotland or Wales. That hadn't always been the case, though. In the Hancock Museum in Newcastle upon Tyne, there had once been a cabinet containing relics from the great days of potshare bowling. Potshare bowling was played mainly by coalminers. It was popular across County Durham and Northumberland throughout the nineteenth and into the twentieth century. As in Ireland, potshare bowling – more commonly called simply 'booling' in the north-east – originally took place on the roads, with competitors trying to complete the course in the fewest throws. Usually the distances were between pubs, giving the sport the feeling of a pedestrian alcoholic steeplechase. Local magistrates gradually outlawed the playing of bowls on public highways and so it moved onto open spaces such as Newcastle's vast Town Moor, Blyth Links, or the beaches at Cambois, Marsden and Hartlepool. On these open spaces, potshare bowls was played on a course called 'the mile' – even though it was reportedly no more than 900 yards long.

The bowls were made from whinstone, using a hammer and file and then ground to a spherical shape in the hollows found in blocks of sandstone. They were then given a shiny coating of pitch. Generally the ball weighed between 15 and 30 ounces. The best players – often stripped down to their long johns – ran up some 20 yards to their mark and then, according to one report, released the ball with a 'long-drawn sigh or grunt'. They could skim it along the surface for 100 yards with a single throw.

The name potshare refers to the fact that the competitors paid an entry fee into a pot and the winner took either the largest share, or often all of it. At its peak, big matches between star bowlers would attract thousands of spectators and a lot of heavy betting. As a consequence, there were numerous attempts to ban it, some because of the danger the ball posed to passers-by, others to the unruliness of the crowds (in 1880 an attempt was made to ban the sport from Town Moor on the grounds of 'blasphemous language').

As in Ireland, each bowler had an assistant called a 'trigger' whose role was to mark where his ball had finished using a 3-inch-long stick called a 'trig'. Marking a spot in this way was likely important when large sums of money had been bet and the temptation must have been high among spectators to help the man they had money resting on by hoofing his opponent's ball back a few yards.

Stakes never matched the levels in Ireland, but they could be large. The *Blyth News* reported on a match between Jack Laws of Cambois (once home of Europe's least likely nudist beach) and Bob Watson of Dudley, played for a stake of £100 a side, the biggest in potshare history. The match took place on Newbiggin Moor in February 1914. The day was so cold both men kept their hands warm by rubbing them with whisky. Watched by an excited crowd of more than 3,000, Laws eventually triumphed on the sixth throw.

Potshare bowling faded from view in the 1930s. In 1949, the *Blyth News* carried a report that local men were planning to revive the sport in East Northumberland. Nothing seems to have come of it.

Many reasons have been advanced for the demise of potshare bowling, from police interference to the rise of football. Perhaps the most convincing of the arguments is that the arrival of the miners' welfare sportsgrounds, with their immaculately tended bowling greens, tempted potshare men away from the moors and beaches with an offer of respectable gentility and cups of tea.

Walking back through Newtonhamilton, with the excitement generated by Mackel's win popping in the air like firecrackers and the sound of celebration burbling from the doorways of the pubs, I was grateful nothing similar had happened to tame the bowlers of Armagh and Cork. The long bullets were well organised, but it still had the feeling of something unregulated and wild. Other sports had been moderated by bureaucrats and sanitised by sponsors. Road bowling still had an outlaw spirit. It was a fox in a world of Labradors.

14

Cheggies and Alleys

CONKERS AND MARBLES, NORTHAMPTONSHIRE AND SUSSEX

It was late September and the conker season was about to reach its grand finale at the World Conker Championship at Ashton in Northamptonshire. Though it was jolly enough, attracting a crowd of 6,000 people from all around the world (the winner of the men's title in 2021 was a Canadian) and raising lots of money for charity, this event always filled me with a sense of melancholy. When my daughter, Maisie, was little, we used to spend the wait for the school bus collecting conkers, or cheggies as they were called in the part of Yorkshire where I grew up.

'When you get home, we could play conkers,' I said the first time we did it.

'What's that?' Maisie asked.

'It's a game,' I explained. 'What you do is punch a hole in

the conker with a screwdriver, thread them on a shoelace and then you whack another person's conker with your conker until you've smashed it to smithereens.'

My daughter considered me carefully, like a golfer assessing a particularly treacherous fairway. 'Yes,' she said eventually. 'We could do that. Or we could plant them in the garden and watch them grow.'

At the time, I thought this highlighted the essential differences between men and women, but when I mentioned it to my daughter fifteen years later, she rolled her eyes and made a pithy comment about gender-stereotyping. The sadness that overcame me when I saw conkers was for the passing of a time when my child couldn't defeat me in an argument.

In truth, the cheggies we'd collected in those days weren't really the fighting kind. They were bulbous and glossy as bodybuilders, and as the great philosopher Nigel 'The Terror of 3B' Molesworth once observed, 'successful conkers are always shrivelled and weedy'. Much like jockeys, in fact. Though, of course, nobody soaks jockeys in vinegar, bakes them in the oven overnight or coats them with clear nail-varnish to improve their performance. Well, not since the authorities got wind of it, anyway.

According to the internet, the first recorded game of conkers was played on the Isle of Wight in 1848. The setting and the date encouraged me to believe it might well have been between Queen Victoria and Prince Albert. I imagine Her Majesty asking her German consort if he would like a quick go at conkers and he, aware by now of the British love of euphemism, willingly agreeing with a slight smile, one that perhaps widened when she added, 'Though due to the disparity in our height, I fear if we are to do it properly we may need a chair.'

Whatever, the World Conker Championships have been held annually since 1965, even surviving the great conker shortage of 2011, which was possibly the greatest threat to the game since the First World War when, instead of playing with their conkers, schoolchildren were encouraged to harvest and deliver them to central government location points as part of the effort to defeat the Kaiser. They were paid seven shillings and sixpence per hundredweight for their efforts. In 1917, more than 3,000 tons of conkers were collected in this manner and shipped to a manufacturer in Kings Lynn. You might wonder why. Well, it turns out conkers contain acetone, which is vital in the production of cordite. Conkers helped win the war.

The World Conker Championships have grown bigger and bigger, and came back strongly after COVID. Not everyone is in favour of them, however. At the start of the millennium, a late-escape holiday auction website carried out a poll which revealed that the majority of people in this country are sick of events that paint a picture of us as a nation of lovable eccentrics. The World Conker Championships, along with the Cooper's Hill Cheese Rolling and the Egremont Crab Fair, were singled out for particular opprobrium. I would stand up firmly in the defence of all three.

Egremont has some claim to being the North's answer to

Robert Dover's Olimpicks. The annual Crab Fair features handicap sprint races, grass track cycling, fell running and Cumberland and Westmorland wrestling. Though it lacks the shin-kicking, it certainly has a harder edge to it than the Cotswolds version. The first time I attended back in 1996, I had taken my dog, Ingo, with me. Ingo was a standard schnauzer with the bristling grey whiskers of a nineteenth-century Prussian general and the muscular shoulders of a javelin thrower. While I was standing watching my daughter riding on a merry-go-round, two shaven-headed men in rugby league shirts approached me and began fussing over Ingo. 'Nice dog,' one of them said, squeezing his neck. 'Strong bugger, isn't he?'

I said he was. I said he pulled so much on his lead that my mother said taking him out for a walk was like wrestling with a bear. The man who had been patting Ingo stood up. He looked me in the eye. 'Does he scrap?' he asked casually. I told him he didn't, that he was as soft as cake dough, though not as sweetly scented. 'Pity,' the bloke said with a scowl. 'There could have been some money in it for you.' And with that, he and his pal sauntered off past a hot dog stand and out of sight. Thinking about it still sends a shudder through me. Perhaps I'm wrong, but I have a feeling nobody would offer you a dog fight in Chipping Camden.

The next time I went to Egremont Crab Fair, I travelled on the train. A couple of decades had gone by and Ingo had long since departed. It was a filthy day in mid-September. The train from Carlisle rolled along the fringe of the Solway Firth and down the coast, rain the consistency of mucus splotting against the windows. We passed chemical plants, vast industrial dairies, the Sellafield nuclear waste centre and rows of houses rendered in a colour that squats grimly in the no man's land between grey and brown. The Irish Sea looked like the contents of a slop bucket. Across from me, two Estuarine walkers in head-to-toe rainwear ate sausage rolls and stared out of the window.

'You been here before?' the woman asked. The man shook his head in response, cheeks bulging with meat and pastry. The woman glanced quickly from left to right. 'Bit bleak, isn't it?' she whispered. The man grinned ruefully, nodded and stuffed more food in his mouth.

Bit bleak. To be honest, even the most patriotic Northerner would find it hard to disagree with her. This part of the north-west is one of England's forgotten corners, a part of Cumbria you're unlikely ever to find yourself in unless you get lost when leaving the Lake District. I got off at St Bees, where the Victorian public school looked like it was auditioning for a role in a TV adaptation of *Decline and Fall* and the general store had a mammoth window display of Trill budgie seed, and caught a bus to Egremont.

Egremont Crab Fair dates back to 1267, when the tenants organised a feast to celebrate having paid their annual rents to the lord of the manor, Lord de Lucy, and he responded generously by sending the revellers a cartload of crab apples for their dinner. Since crab apples are pretty much inedible unless made into jelly, this was perhaps an ironic gesture from his lordship. Perhaps in equally sarcastic tribute, the fair became an annual event, surviving the de Lucy family, who fell foul of the Tudors and had their lands confiscated and the castle in Egremont reduced to a ruin.

These days, the apples at the crab fair are supplied by a local supermarket and are a type that can be eaten without the need to boil them with sugar and strain them through one of those strange conical sieves first. At Egremont Crab Fair, you can see many once-popular entertainments, such as climbing the greasy pole to win a leg of mutton, foot races through the streets and, most famously, gurning (or face-pulling).

Gurning was once a feature of most British horse fairs, particularly those in the Midlands. Nowadays, though, Egremont is the last bastion of competitive face-pulling. The event that day saw many elderly and wild-looking men and women removing their false teeth, sticking their heads through a horse collar (known as a braffin) and contorting their faces into the shapes that call to mind a French bulldog chewing a wasp. It was held in the Market Hall. By the time the gurning started, the crowd has already been whipped into a frenzy by a junior talent contest (strangely stuffed with kids imitating Norman Wisdom and Frank Spencer, two people they could surely only have known through other people doing impressions of them) and a pipe-smoking race in which competitors puffed through wads of thick-twist tobacco in the sort of time it takes most pipe-smokers to cough up a ball of phlegm. The audience then went ballistic as competitors young and old, male and female, contorted their mugs into the weirdest shapes they could manage and were scored on their efforts by a panel of judges. The scene might well be described as Brueghelian, though 'nuts' would do just as well.

For some reason, this ancient activity had annoyed those surveyed by the Late-escape holiday auction website. According to a site spokesperson, 'with British culture degenerating to game-show level, it is hardly surprising that Britons feel humiliated'.

Though there is a self-conscious wackiness about some of the events that can be irritating (how many more times do we need to see prop forwards from the local rugby club dressed as Charlie's Angels before we cry 'Enough!'?) it has to be said that if the British people find the World Bog Snorkelling Championship makes them cringe, how must they feel when they see Boris Johnson's suit? Or indeed Boris Johnson?

Everywhere, though, it seems the game of conkers is under threat. The newspapers report that scout leaders in Windsor and Eton have banned cubs from playing without written consent from their parents because the game is considered too dangerous. In Norwich, a row of horse chestnut trees was cut down because the local council judged the falling conkers to be a hazard to passers-by.

The future King Charles spoke out against the action at the time, and rightly so. His Majesty must fear for the sanity of a society that values sharp cognitive faculties more highly than interesting head wounds.

Not that I am unqualified in my support of the World Conker Championships, I should say. At Ashton, they play the three-hits-each rule. Personally, I favour the hit-till-you-miss style of my schooldays, which to my mind gives a more subtle game.

All aficionados know that, when it comes to conkers, hitting is much the same as being hit, Newton's third law of motion stating that action and reaction are equal. With hit-till-you-miss, the owner of a delicate conker, or one that has been reduced to a shard of shell no bigger than a toad's toupée, can preserve it by administering only the softest of taps to his adversary's nut until darkness or boredom intervenes to save him.

Nor does the Ashton competition include 'stamps', an exciting variation which allows the opponent of anyone whose conker hits the ground to chase after it, attempting to crush it under foot, while the owner scrabbles about on the floor trying to retrieve it and avoid getting his or her fingers broken.

You might think it unlikely that anyone would drop their conker during a competition, but a gifted player can use 'strings' (a shot in which the respective conker laces become entwined) to disarm their adversary with a sudden twirl of the wrist in the manner of D'Artagnan. Or at least he can unless his opponent has wound the lace round his fist.

In this case, any attempt to spin or tug the conker from his grasp simply draws the lace around the knuckles until they are as tight as a tourniquet. On a frosty autumn morning, this produces the kind of sharp, icy pain traditionally associated with unrequited love. Or supporting Yorkshire County Cricket Club.

The winning conker, of course, inherits all the previous victories of the defeated nut. If a two-er beats a six-er, it becomes an eight-er and so on. I can't help thinking this scoring system might profitably be adopted by other sports. Imagine the thrills and drama that would be brought to the Premiership if the winners not only picked up three points for a victory but also all their beaten opponents' points too.

Another annual event that had aggravated those who spoke of 'theme park Britain' is the World Marbles Championships, which was first held outside the Greyhound Inn at Tinsley Green in East Sussex in 1932. In recent years, the championships have been dominated by teams from Germany. The best of them were the Saxonia Globe Snippers who regularly beat off the challenge of English sides to become Marbles Team World Champions (or Murmel-Weltmeister Mannschaft, as they say in Germany). After they took the title for the second consecutive year in 2003, the Snippers' spokesman, Andreas Haldebrandt, pronounced, 'We are very happy', words that suggested he would be celebrating with half a pretzel and a small glass of milk. Meanwhile, one of the world championship organisers blamed the poor performance of our native marbles players on all-too-familiar failings. 'Too much beer and not enough practice,' said Julia McCarthy-Fox.

Marbles is an ancient sport. Ovid wrote about it, Brueghel painted it. Sussex is one of its spiritual centres. The world championships began in nearby Copthorne, moving to Tinsley Green shortly afterwards. The region has produced some of the sport's true greats, men such as Jim 'Atomic Thumb'

Longhurst, a gardener from Slaugham who back in the 1940s would astonish fans by shattering a beer mug from 4 feet away with a powerful flick of his tolley (the marbles equivalent of the cue ball); Sam Spooner, the Sussex cowherd who used the same tolley for forty-five years and is credited with being one of the first men to swear on British radio when he blurted a quick 'bloody' during an episode of *In Town Tonight* in 1946; and the diminutive Welshman, Wee Willie Wright, who won the world title five times in the 1950s and always kept a hot-water bottle in his coat to stop his right thumb from stiffening up between knuckle-downs in the 6-foot ring.

These men were giants of the Sussex style of marbles known as Ring Taw, in which competitors use a tolley to try to knock marbles out of the ring. Where I grew up, we played a simpler and more brutal game. In this, the first player threw down his marble and the second tried to hit and move it. If he did, he got to keep it. If not, the first player took his turn to try to hit and budge his opponent's marble.

Fast and furious, this was a quick way of losing your marbles. An unwary child could step into the infant school's playground with his pocket money's worth of shiny new glass alleys on Monday morning and find, by the time the bell rang for assembly, he or she had nothing left but the plastic net bag they bought them in. The reason for this was simple. While the neophytes came armed with marbles made from glass or pot, the top kids only used steel ball bearings, or doshers as they were known.

Doshers of any size gave a player a distinct advantage over ordinary marbles. But while most children were usually only able to locate small doshers (known as tipsies) by prising them from the catch on an airing cupboard door using a screwdriver, those of us lucky enough to have relatives working in heavy industry could get our hands on industrial ball bearings. I recall having one my dad brought home from British Steel that was the size of a squash ball. Even a direct hit from a few inches away couldn't budge it a millimetre. Atomic Thumb Longhurst in his pomp would have struggled to defeat me, I can tell you.

15

Tap and Slap

BAT AND TRAP, KENT

When I was a youth, I was a keen member of the Young Ornithologists' Club, spending many happy weekends at Seal Sands on Teesside wiping rain off my binoculars. These days, the only twitching I do is when I fall asleep in a chair, but I can still identify the woodpecker by its undulating flight and the buzzard by its mewing call. I never really got the hang of trees, though. I'm no good on trees and I'm only marginally better when it comes to flowers.

After I got back from my stoolball expedition, I went for a walk with a friend and her daughter. We went up an old green lane between high stands of hawthorn and cow parsley. 'Oh, that's Jack-by-the-hedge,' my friend said whenever her daughter asked what a white flower was. 'Are you sure?' I invariably replied. 'I think it looks more like lady's smock.'

If I asked my dad, who's from Lancashire, what the same

flower was, in all likelihood he'd cock his head slightly to one side, squint and say, 'Now, I think that's old man's beard.' My mother would interject. 'Well, I don't know what they call it where *he* comes from, but in the North Riding we always know it as meadow custards.'

Lord Chesterfield, the eighteenth-century wit and writer, took great exception to the idea that English spelling should be standardised. 'I am a gentleman,' he thundered at the pedants who lined up to scrawl red ink over his manuscripts, 'and I shall spell words how I damn well choose.' I feel his lordship's commendable attitude (which was much like T. H. White's to darts) should have been expanded to cover the naming of flowers. At one time, every plant had a multitude of names. Then, at some point, a self-appointed busybody had decided what they all ought really to be called and started lecturing everyone else. Who it was I have no idea, but he or she certainly had some front, if you ask me.

It is my conviction that beyond the obvious – bluebells, cowslips, primroses, wild violets, wood anemones – most people know the names of around half a dozen wildflowers and dole them out them according to shape and colour. If it is pink and has petals, I will say 'campion' and somebody else will say, 'Actually I think that's ragged robin.'

'Campion is what we call it in the north-east,' I'll reply.

I feel I am on safe ground playing the regional card. When it came to wild plants, the homogenisers have not succeeded quite so well as they did with spelling and punctuation. Names still change according to where you are. Where I grew up, that long gummy green weed with the little balls on it that glue themselves to dogs' fur was called grewgrass. Others call it goosegrass, while Northumbrians refer to it as sticky jack.

The only people I've ever met who genuinely do seem to know the 'proper' names of wildflowers are my mother's maiden aunts. 'Now that,' they'd say, 'is shepherd's purse and next to it is tufted vetch. Oh, and look, a little patch of hare's-foot trefoil surrounding a viper's bugloss.' The names of wildflowers I should say are infinitely more elaborate and poetic than the plants themselves, most of which look like something a spider doodled.

Sometimes, though, even the aunts couldn't identify things. 'I don't think it is hedge bedstraw,' they'd say. 'The leaves aren't right. And it's definitely not mouse-ear chickweed . . .'

'Well,' my father would comment, 'my guess would be tinker's nutbag, but I'm not sure we get that in this part of the North Riding.'

When it came to games, bat and trap is very much in the wildflower category. There are dozens of names for it across Britain. These include tribet, buck stick, spell-and-ore, trounce holes, and trippit and coit. In Shropshire – where it was called dog stick – the game was apparently played by young men on Shrove Tuesday. In Bury St Edmunds, it was called trap ball and played on Shrove Tuesday, Easter Monday and Whitsuntide. A chronicler of the local scene quoted by the folklorist Alice Gomme tells us that 'twelve older women side off for a game at "Trap and Ball" which is kept up with the greatest spirit and vigour until sunset', while Chambers'

Book of Days reports a similar custom among the cowmen of Chester.

In the far fringes of West Yorkshire and on the eastern edge of Lancashire, the game is called knur and spell. My first encounter with knur and spell came via a report on Yorkshire Television news that featured Fred Trueman, then at his *Indoor League* Yorkieness-turned-to-eleven peak, and a horde of men in unlikely headgear who all spoke with such cask-conditioned West Riding accents that they made the Tetley Bittermen from the TV beer adverts sound like Dame Barbara Cartland.

Knur and spell is the Tasmanian devil of British traditional pastimes. No sooner has its extinction been announced than a report comes in from some remote corner of Yorkshire or Lancashire of the distinctive sound of sycamore on clay and the sight of a white 'potty' flying through the Pennine air.

The ancient game of knur and spell is as resilient as the land it's played on. It has been around for more than a thousand years, brought to Britain by the Vikings. It's a lot like golf, though perhaps since fastidiousness wasn't much prized on a long ship, the winner is not the player who strikes the ball with patient accuracy, but the one who whacks it hardest and furthest. Not that the game lacks its subtleties. 'There's a lot to it,' observed former world champion Len Kershaw. 'Judging the wind, the right trajectory and the lay of the land.'

The game was popular across Georgian England, but in the latter half of the nineteenth century its heartlands narrowed to the hilly border between West Yorkshire and east

Lancashire, in villages with names like Foulridge, Stainland, Baildon and Greetland that hint at toughness and tragedy.

The knur is the ball. Originally made from wood or leather, in the Victorian age it was replaced by the glazed clay marbles used to descale copper kettles. These were known as 'potties'. In the 1970s, when electric kettles became the norm, production of the china balls ceased, and an appeal for donations from the organiser of knur and spell's annual world championship inspired the national newspaper headline 'Shortage of potties causes crisis in Yorkshire'.

The spell was originally a strip of wood balanced over a peg. Tapping one end popped the knur into the air to be struck with the club-headed 'pummel', which resembles a golf driver. This simple spell gave way to a spring-loaded metal contraption. Not all players use the spell, however. Many, particularly in Lancashire, favoured a 'pin' – a wooden frame and arm, something like a miniature gallows, from which the knur is suspended in a string noose. Fierce arguments rage on which style is the harder, but then voluble debate is an integral part of the game. 'The players were always rowing over the rules,' said Herbert Bateson, a veteran observer of the sport, 'but they could never meet and sort things out. They were all deadly enemies.'

Since a potty can be struck a fair distance – the world record, set by Joe Machin of Grinnersdale in 1899, is 304 yards – the high pastures of the dales are the favoured venue. The ball is smacked over drystone walls and across tussocked grass. Sometimes a player gets a lucky bounce from a rock,

NO PIE, NO PRIEST

at other times his potty sticks in a cowpat. These are not the sort of things that trouble Tiger Woods.

A potty is sized between a golf ball and a glass alley. Locating one in rough ground isn't easy and, since any that aren't found within five minutes are disallowed, some players had terriers trained to find them. The dogs' job is sometimes made more difficult by unscrupulous players who pay off spectators to stand on a rival's potty and squash it beneath the mud.

Heavy betting encouraged such sharp practice. In the 1930s, games were played for big money in front of crowds of 10,000 people. In a Pathé newsreel from 1933, Jim Crenshaw, a champion from Yorkshire, offered to take on all-comers for a £200 stake – this at a time when an English top-flight footballer earned £8 per week.

In 1969, when I'd seen that Yorkshire TV broadcast of the world championship, complete with commentary from Fiery Fred in an astrakhan hat that looked even more man-made than his hair, 5,000 fans turned up to watch and tens of thousands more tuned in at home. At that point, there were mutterings of the sport seeking Olympic status. It proved a high point. By the 1990s, players, spectators, sponsors and F. S. Trueman had drifted elsewhere. At the start of the new millennium, knur and spell was reported to have disappeared for good, only to resurface on BBC's *Countryfile* in 2011. There were matches at the Silsdon and Cowling galas in 2015, and at Bradley Show two years later. Since then, things have gone quiet again, although given the game's obdurate refusal to die, it seems likely that somewhere in Pendle or Calderdale a potty is skimming across a moor top even as you read this.

Knur and spell – and other games such as nipsy (played around Barnsley with an egg-shaped hardwood ball and a club made from a pick-axe handle), peggy (a game involving a short length of wood struck with a club that was played in Cumbria by, among others, a young Stan Laurel) and billets (a 4-foot-long club used to whack a ball that looked vaguely like a wilted banana) – all involved trying to smash the ball (or a lump of wood) as far as you could. Bat and trap – and its ancestor trap ball – is different. Here the aim is to score points. Hitting the ball accurately rather than hard is the emphasis. In fact, whacking a ball mightily is likely to get a player caught out, or barred. In trap ball, a simple wooden 'trap' flicks the ball up into the air and it is struck 'on the volley' by the batter using what looks a little like a sawn-off table tennis bat.

Like most sports, trap ball was frowned upon by organised religion. In the mid-seventeenth century, John Bunyan was playing a game of bat and trap when he heard the voice of God telling him to renounce his sins. Whether trap ball was one of them goes unrecorded, but Bunyan gave up the game nonetheless.

Nor did trap ball find much favour with Joseph Strutt, who sneered that it was a 'childish pastime when compared with cricket'. (Of knur and spell, which he called Northern Spell, Strutt is even more dismissive. 'This pastime possesses but little variety and is by no mean as amusing to bystanders as cricket or trap-ball.' So there.)

Despite its 'childishness', or maybe because of it, trap ball became rather fashionable among wealthy young gents in Regency England. It was championed by George, Prince of Wales, who played in matches on the Level in Brighton, where the game is still commemorated in the name of the Bat and Ball pub and played every Easter.

Trap ball seems to have been popular across the country in some form or other, but gradually faded away until, by the start of the twentieth century, Canterbury was the principal – and possibly the only – centre of the sport. The author Timothy Finn attributes this to 'an unselfconscious interest from players and an organised competitive league', to which he adds the charm and beauty of the cathedral city.

I had thought this latter comment a little far-fetched. After all, most sport generally thrives in places that are grim and ugly, rough and unseemly. Diego Maradona nearly drowned as a child in an uncovered cesspit a few yards from his home, while the great Filipino boxer Manny Pacquiao laughed off talk that British opponent Ricky Hatton had endured a poverty-stricken childhood by saying, 'When I was a kid, my father killed our pet dog and ate it.' The notion that sport might be nurtured by the loveliness of an environment seemed plain wrong to me. That was until I walked into St Stephen's Green in Canterbury and saw the Ye Olde Beverlie pub.

Built from salmon-pink brick, bow-fronted, with white-framed windows, it was a public house that seemed to have sprung straight from the illustrations of Arthur Rackham.

You could imagine Badger and Ratty propping up the burnished oak bar, and Mr Toad excitedly capering about on the shining clay-tiled floor.

Ye Olde Beverlie has been hosting bat and trap matches since 1570, and the bat and trap club was founded way back in around 1730. It's a measure of how old and well established it was that the Beverley Cricket Club, which was considered to be almost as old as the illustrious Hambledon of Richard Nyren, was widely believed to be an offshoot of the bat and trap club. In 1950, John Arlott commentated on a game at Ye Olde Beverlie for a special BBC radio broadcast about the Roman Road to Canterbury. Arlott gave the history of the game and – according to reports – became livelier after helping himself to regular swigs from a glass of 'a refreshing beverage' he had placed on the scorer's table.

I imagine that Arlott, who was almost as fond of the English countryside as he was of Beaujolais, would have enjoyed his evening at Ye Olde Beverlie. It would have been hard not to. Indeed, the thought of playing a game in the garden here, then retiring to the bar afterwards for a pint of Shepherd Neame IPA, filled me with such enthusiasm that had it not been for the fact that I lived 350 miles away, I'd have joined the bat and trap club and paid my subs immediately.

As it was, I settled for a drink. There was no bat and trap at Ye Olde Beverlie that night, so I headed off to Canterbury bus station. This lacked the obvious charms of Ye Olde Beverlie but opened up the romantic promise of trips to Dumpton, Hoath, Seasalter and Stelling Minnis. I caught the bus known as the

Triangle, which carried me north through the suburbs to the village of Broad Oak. Here a seventeenth-century thatched cottage, an oasthouse and a duck pond further convinced me that I had entered a picture-book illustration of life in an English village. Before I could get too dewy-eyed, however, some lads in one of those little-wheeled cars with an engine that sounds like they stole it from a Chieftain tank raced past, bass booming so loudly from the inside that they made the giblets of watching birds vibrate. This was modern rural life as I knew it. If they were anything like my local youth, they'd be off to park up in some local beauty spot and litter the grass verge with nitrous oxide cylinders, the little scamps.

The Golden Lion in Broad Oak had been one of the founder members of the Canterbury Bat and Trap League back in 1922, although they didn't actually play a competitive match until the following year. Photos showed the team from the inaugural season sitting proudly on the pitch, their ranks filled with men from a local family named Keem.

The pub was another brick beauty with a picket fence, Whitstable Bay beer on draught and a sun-dappled garden at the back where the bat and trap pitches were laid. The fielding side could shelter from the heat in what looked like a rustic bus shelter, while the batting team loitered in the shade of the trees. There was a wooden playhouse off to the left of it and, in between, a snicket gate into a well-tended vegetable garden. The scorers – one from each team – were housed in a neat sentry box. The grass of the pitch was immaculately mowed in a series of stripes and as flat as a golf green.

Tonight's game was a league fixture in the Canterbury and District Premier Division, sponsored by a local tree surgeon. The Golden Lion were taking on one of the powerhouses of the game, The Artichoke, whose pub-home was a glorious half-timbered sixteenth-century place in the village of Chartham which, aside from its predictable bucolic glory, was also home to one of the last remaining tracing-paper mills in Britain. The 'Chokes success rested to some degree on one family, the Snows, three generations of whom were in the current starting line-up. They were top of the table, with four wins out of five. The home side had managed just one victory in their five fixtures. It looked like a mismatch, but the home side proved as resilient as a twice-baked conker and held their own for much of the evening.

The version of trap ball played in Kent differs from its many variants in one important particular: it has a 'wicket' that must be hit to get a batter out. This, and the fact that the pitch is a similar length to that of cricket (21 yards as against 22), has led some people to suggest that England's summer game might actually have evolved from it. It seems more likely, though, that – as with stoolball – the two sports evolved side by side. The width of the field, inside which the fielders must stand and the batter hit the ball, is 13 1/2 feet, a distance marked with boundary posts that look like the sort of things that normally hold up a washing line.

In early incarnations, the trap was made from an old shoe that was turned upside down. A hole was carved in the heel for the ball to rest in and the bat tapped down on the toe to flick it up into the air. Bats were made from larch and the ball from boxwood. These days, the trap is about 2 foot long with a narrow piece of wood – the striker – pivoted on the centre like a see-saw. The ball is placed in a hollow at one end. The batter bangs the opposite end, catapulting the ball a few feet into the air. He then hits it. His aim is to get the ball between the two boundary posts without being caught by a fielder. If he is caught, misses the ball entirely, strikes it wide of the posts or hits it seven or more feet over the posts, he is out. If none of these occur, he steps aside while a member of the fielding team bowls the ball underarm back at the 5-inch-square white 'wicket' on the front of the trap. From 21 yards, hitting this tiny target is tricky. If the fielder misses, the batter scores one run; if the fielder hits, the batter is out. If a run is recorded, the batter is free to strike again. In batting, high scores for individuals nudge up towards the half-century, while a bowler who hits the trap three times will earn himself a congratulatory pat on the back and a jug of beer. Teams are made up of eight players. After they have all batted, the runs are totalled and the team with the most is the winner of that leg. Games are played over three legs.

There are two methods of hitting the ball in bat and trap. One is to stand off to the side, crouching in the manner of somebody delivering a bowls wood, and smack it as you would a serve in table tennis. The other is to stand with your feet on either side of the trap, holding the bat two-handed. It put me in mind of a big industrial kitchen in which I'd once worked as a commis chef, where we'd occasionally fill a spare few minutes by hurling apples at each other while wielding frying pans.

The obvious disadvantage of the latter method, or so it seemed to me, was that you were likely to scoop the ball into the hands of a fielder. Even more worrying, if you banged the trap too hard, the ball would fly up and crack you on the nose. The fact that during the course of the game neither of these things happened attests to the aptitude of the players. In 1946, the *Thanet Advertiser* claimed that bat and trap required 'the skills of a bowls player, the eye of a baseball player and the accuracy of a tennis player combined'. I'm not sure I'd go that far, but there was more involved than initially met the eye. Yet, while skill and experience would play a part in becoming a good player, bat and trap also seemed like the sort of sport even the rank beginner could enjoy. In that sense, it seemed more like badminton rather than tennis. Players didn't need a degree of competence to produce a competitive game.

Like Aunt Sally, bat and trap was a late bloomer. Indeed, it probably wouldn't have made any inroads onto the English rural scene at all if it hadn't been for a chap named Bill Humphries who, in the early 1920s, codified the rules and somehow persuaded six publicans to set up pitches outside their premises. In May 1922, the Canterbury and District Bat and Trap League was launched with five teams based at pubs in Canterbury – including Ye Olde Beverlie – alongside the Golden Lion. By 1930, the league had expanded to fourteen teams spread over two divisions. The clubs were mainly associated with pubs, though there were some works teams, including Post Office Internal and External, and the Gas and Waterworks.

Jakey Janes – a keen player who also handles social media for the league – explains that one of the reasons bat and trap became popular in the 1920s was because wounded service-men coming back from the First World War could play the game. 'There were a lot of maimed soldiers in Kent. You can bat and bowl even if you've only got one arm,' he says. I mention that stoolball enjoyed a revival in Sussex for just the same reasons. 'I can see that. Obviously in bat and trap there's no running around either, so it was a good way for disabled men to get out in the fresh air and the sunshine.'

I mention the dangers of the popped-up ball. 'Oh yes,' he says, 'I've seen quite a few black eyes. We even had a broken nose last season.'

In 1951, the league introduced a rule that all bat and trap pitches must be fitted with floodlights. This was quite an innovation. It would be another four years before the Football Association allowed competitive matches to be played under lights and they wouldn't become a mandatory ground requirement in the Football League until the late 1960s. Indeed, bat and trap floodlit fixtures were such a novelty that, in 1954, the BBC filmed a game and showed it on the nine o'clock news.

The reason floodlights were necessary for bat and trap was that most of the players were agricultural workers. In summer months, they worked late, so it was common for matches of bat and trap to begin at a point in the evening when many people in the rest of Britain were having a supper of Ovaltine and digestive biscuits. Like moths, players seem to have been attracted by the lights and the popularity of the game soared. In 1952, a ladies division was added and then expanded to three divisions. By 1982, the league had eighty teams spread across eight divisions.

There were many more teams clamouring to join, but the CDL's administrators felt they had reached capacity. After a good deal of heated argument, the teams that had been refused membership formed a breakaway league of their own – the East Kent Friendly League (the Friendly part of that name seems to have been a snarky dig at the Canterbury administrators), which soon had close to twenty teams. These were mixed-gender sides; once again, bat and trap was ahead of the curve.

Soon there was a third league in Sevenoaks, which also had close to twenty clubs. Perhaps as a consequence, the Canterbury and District League shrank down to thirty-nine men's teams, with a separate division for ladies. Other leagues opened across Kent until, by the end of the 1980s, there were around 4,000 people playing bat and trap each week in about sixty pubs.

Not that it had all been cakes and ale. In 1954, bat and trap – just like knur and spell – had been hit by a ball crisis. Bill Humphries told the *Kentish Express* that the league had only a dozen rubber balls of the required size left and these were being 'jealously guarded'. Before the Second World War, the league had balls made in batches of 100 but after the conflict, firms claimed they could not make fewer than 1,000 per batch. Some clubs had taken to using lacrosse balls, much to Humphries' disgust as the ball was supposed to be 2 1/4 inches in diameter. 'The [lacrosse balls] are 2 1/2 inches in diameter and as such make both batting and bowling easier,' he said. A week later, a retired Indian Army officer wrote to Humphries with details of a firm in the sub-continent that would make bat and trap balls for him at a fraction of the price charged by British firms. The disaster was averted. Nowadays, the sort of hard rubber ball you throw for a dog is used.

I sat on a wooden bench in the Golden Lion's garden and watched. The game moved along at a decent pace, but it was hardly strenuous. Since there's nothing to be gained from power, batting is gentle, while the throw back at the wicket is delivered along the ground underarm, like a bowls wood. Old film from the 1950s shows the teams wearing three-piece suits, the batters approaching the trap with their pipes clamped in their mouths. It's a game you could play while eating a sandwich, which to some people would rule it out of being sport, but since I've played in many football matches where people did just that – and plenty of cricket matches where the batter came out with a fag in his mouth – I'm not among them.

The game seems sociable, but there's a definite edge to it. 'It's very competitive,' Janes says. The game has just about weathered COVID. 'We had thirty-one teams in 2019 and we've got thirty now, so it's not bad,' he says. There are also signs of a renewed interest. 'We've had enquiries from six potential new clubs. A couple of them are football teams who want something to do in the summer. I think that's a good way forward for us. There are quite a lot of young players, but that will bring in more.'

Janes has no explanation for why bat and trap has never spread from Kent. It's not for want of effort on his part. Like stoolball pioneer William Wilson Grantham, Janes is an enthusiastic promoter of his sport. He has even tried to take the game global. 'I wrote to all the nine towns that are twinned with Canterbury – Reims, Mölndal in Sweden, the Hungarian place, Esztergom, the lot. I thought we could get a little international tournament together. But I never heard anything back from any of them.'

The Golden Lion team performed decently before going down 2-1. There were growls of praise in accents that seemed more south London than rural burr and a good deal of chuckling. As the light began to fade, bats appeared and flitted between the houses in search of food. Glasses tinkled in the bar and the smell of ale and chips wafted by on the warm breeze.

Somewhere to the south, vast queues of traffic were lining up at Dover in a Brexit-related passport crisis. The war in Ukraine rumbled on. The price of fuel had soared. There were rail and postal strikes, and dire warnings in the press of power blackouts and food shortages. The ice caps were melting. I thought about the Latin American restaurateur fleeing Blackpool and the wounded servicemen returning home from the mud and bloodshed of Flanders. Anatole France had written that the playing of games was about 'laughter and forgetting'. Disaster was looming on the horizon, a dark shadow next to the setting sun, yet sitting here in the garden of the Golden Lion with a pint of good beer, the pat of ball on bat, the gurgle of laugher and the buttery light of late summer melting beyond the trees, everything on our little island seemed alright.

ACKNOWLEDGEMENTS

Many people spoke to me of their chosen games with knowledge, pride and enthusiasm. High among them were Tom Monaghan, Andrew Lusted, Jakey Janes, Andy Smart, Bob Johnson, Tom Parker, Sheila Thompson, John Ferguson, Alex Fotheringham and Richard Macdonald. Many books have been consulted along the way including Joseph Strutt's *Sports and Pastimes of the People of England*, Alice B. Gomme's *The Traditional Games of England, Scotland and Ireland*, *Pub Games of England* by Timothy Finn, *Played at the Pub* by Arthur Taylor, *Uppies and Doonies* by Hugh Hornby, *The Story of Bowls* edited by Phil Pilley, *In Search of Food* by David and Richard Mabey, *The Shinty Year Book*, *The World History of Highland Games* by David Webster, *Road Bowling in Ireland* by Brian Toal, *Bowls, Skittles and Quoits* by 'Skipper', *Turnpike Road to Tartan Track* by Frederick Moffatt and *The Glynde Butterflies 1866–1887* by Andrew Lusted.

Finally, I would like to thank the British railway system. Many years ago, a friend of mine who was a chef commented that 'you can't cook properly unless you're in a fury'. I feel the same way about writing. Luckily, during my travels in 2021 and 2022, our trains provided me with enough fuel to power me through the rest of what passes for my career.